The Historic
Country Hotels of England

A Select Guide

WENDY ARNOLD

The Historic
Country Hotels of England

A Select Guide

With 120 color photographs by
ROBIN MORRISON

An Owl Book
Holt, Rinehart and Winston
New York

For Mick

On the cover: medieval Buckland Manor, in one of the loveliest parts of the Cotswolds, is among the finest hotels in England. See p.49.

Frontispiece: A liveried hall-porter waits to take up your luggage at the gracious wrought-iron gates of Middlethorpe Hall, near York. See p.21.

Opposite: Dinner is laid at the Lake District hotel Miller Howe. The walls of the dining room were painted by the Italian artist Stefano Ficalbi in 1979. See p.17.

Copyright © 1985 by Thames and Hudson Ltd.

All rights reserved, including the right to reproduce this book or portions thereof in any form.

Published by Holt, Rinehart and Winston,
383 Madison Avenue,
New York, New York 10017.

Library of Congress Cataloging in Publication Data

Arnold, Wendy
   The historic country hotels of England.

      1. Hotels, taverns, etc.—England—Directories.
I. Title.
TX910.G7A66   1984   647′.944201   84-25144
ISBN: 0-03-004133-3 (An Owl bk.) (pbk.)

First American edition published in hardcover by
Holt, Rinehart and Winston in 1985.

First Owl Book Edition—1986

Designer: Geoffrey Penna
Printed in Italy

10 9 8 7 6 5 4 3 2 1

ISBN 0-03-004133-3

Contents

Preface

A romantic view of Le Talbooth, a luxury retreat in the very heart of Constable country. See p. 35.

English country house hotels, like American country inns, have enormous personality and charm, and are as individual and interesting as their owners. They can be vast, elegant, formal mansions standing in many acres of parkland, or tiny thatched cottages staffed by local village girls. Some claim to have ghosts; some are castles; some will organize pheasant shooting or trout fishing; some are run by families whose ancestors have lived in them for four centuries or more; above all, most are people's homes.

I wrote this book because, as an English woman living in the USA, I was frequently asked by American friends for information about the best and most historic country hotels in England. In the past thirty years my husband's career in the oil business has led me to set up home in Arabia, South and Central America and Africa. We have done a great deal of international travelling and I could tell friends of the merits – or otherwise – of the Meurice in Paris, the Hassler in Rome, the Mamounia in Marrakesh or the Cairo Sheraton, but I felt out of touch with English country house hotels. On my next trip to England I drove out into the countryside to investigate. Some hotels were a delight, others (equally warmly recommended by leading guides) were a disaster. Intrigued and challenged, I decided to discover the true state of things.

After six months of hard work, cross-referencing all the hotel guidebooks I could find on both sides of the Atlantic, I narrowed my choice to the two hundred which sounded most promising. I wrote for their brochures, went to see them, and stayed at the ones I liked the look of. I did not tell the owners that I was working on a book until after I had paid the bill, so that I would not receive any favors or special treatment, but could observe their level of hospitality to a middle-aged lady travelling alone.

I looked for hotels that were historically or architecturally interesting, in lovely countryside, with marvellous chefs, and delightful décor. The owners had to be warmly welcoming and everything had to be efficiently run, so that everywhere was spotlessly clean, service was rapid, bedrooms were comfortable and tastefully furnished and bathrooms excellent, with plenty of hot water. Most importantly, they had to be places where everybody CARED. There seemed little point in staying anywhere, no matter how quaint, where I would pay to be less comfortable than at home. Maintaining high standards in what is often a very old building, training local staff and coping with the English weather make great demands on the owners, who have often retired from other careers – merchant bankers, accountants, food guide inspectors – but who share a great love of their homes.

On my travels I rediscovered the pleasures of the English countryside: innumerable ancient villages and their churches, gardens great and small, stately homes. I found to my joy – and somewhat to my surprise – that there is excellent food to be eaten all over England, prepared by a new generation of young English chefs. Even the pubs, whose imagination had not previously stretched beyond a ploughman's bread and cheese lunch, are now serving fresh salads and country specialities.

Each hotel is quite different from all the others, but they can all be reached in a day's drive from London. They are conveniently spaced for a leisurely tour right round England if one wishes, and there is a selection in each area to suit one's purpose in going to that part of the country. If you want to be pampered and cosseted in enormous luxury; to stay in a historic house with an interesting history; or to find a pleasant base for sightseeing and exploring the countryside, the hotels in this book are for you. The best of the English country house hotels give one the feeling of staying with welcoming friends. Of the many hotels I visited, these are the thirty I most enjoyed.

General Information

Preparation Booking is essential for all the hotels described, and should be done as far in advance as possible. As ideas of comfort vary, be very specific about special requirements. If you travel with a lot of luggage and need a large room, if stairs are a problem and you need a ground floor room, if you are travelling with friends and want accommodation similar to theirs, if you cannot live without a wall-mounted shower or a six-feet wide double bed, say so when booking. (Americans are always amazed to find how few luxury hotels in England have showers as a standard fitting.) Most hotels are extremely helpful about special diets. I found all the owners charming about problems that arose during visits: a free drink was provided while I waited for a jammed lock to be opened, a hot-water bottle and an extra heater were offered when a summer day suddenly turned icy cold, and the chef at one hotel kindly jump-started my car for me while we had a fascinating conversation about his use of herbs!

Terms Since prices can fluctuate, I have given only a rough guideline. The hotels are divided into three categories, based on the price for two people sharing a room for one night and having dinner (without wine) and continental breakfast. I have included Value Added Tax at 15% and service at 10%, although some hotels quote these as a separate charge.

Moderate £70–100 (approx. $85–120)
Medium £101–130 (approx. $121–155)
Expensive £131–180 (approx. $156–215)

This does not include *à la carte* prices, drinks, phone calls, or other extras. Most hotels make a supplementary charge for a full English breakfast. Special bargain weekends, reductions for longer stays, and Christmas programs are sometimes available. Enquire when booking.

Getting there I have included directions and approximate journey times for those travelling by car from London. Some hotels are accessible by train, and owners will provide courtesy cars from the rail station. I have indicated where helicopter landing facilities are available (notice must always be given).

Sightseeing Most hotel owners are both knowledgeable and helpful about sightseeing, and many have prepared maps and guides to their district. I have made a brief selection of the most important attractions in each hotel's surroundings. For those intent on comprehensive sightseeing, *Historic Houses, Castles and Gardens in Great Britain and Ireland*, published annually and available from most book and newspaper stores in the UK, gives a county-by-county list of opening times and admission charges. A small yellow booklet by the National Gardens Scheme, *Gardens Open to the Public*, will fascinate keen gardeners, for it lists those private gardens which open for a few days each year to help charity. These are a great mixture, ranging from the imposing to the humble, but all give many ideas about grouping plants, and often the opportunity to meet their interesting owners. As many of the finest properties in England are owned by the National Trust, it is worth contemplating annual membership of the Trust (available from all Trust properties). This grants free entry and helps to preserve England's heritage.

Eating out Since the smaller hotels usually do not open for lunch, I have suggested under "Refreshments" places to stop for a quick meal. Most are picturesque pubs or small restaurants. It may also be possible to eat there in the evenings. In "Dining Out" I have suggested more elaborate establishments for dinner. Pubs are usually open from midday to 2.30 and from 6.00 in the evening (7.00 on Sundays) until 10.30. (Times can vary in different parts of the country.)

Footnote In a well-run hotel there should be few problems, and I am confident that the owners of those I have chosen will be concerned about their guests and helpful and courteous at all times. Should there be any difficulties, or indeed any specially pleasant surprises, please let me know by writing to me, care of the publishers.

An alphabetical index of hotels and their locations appears on page 96.

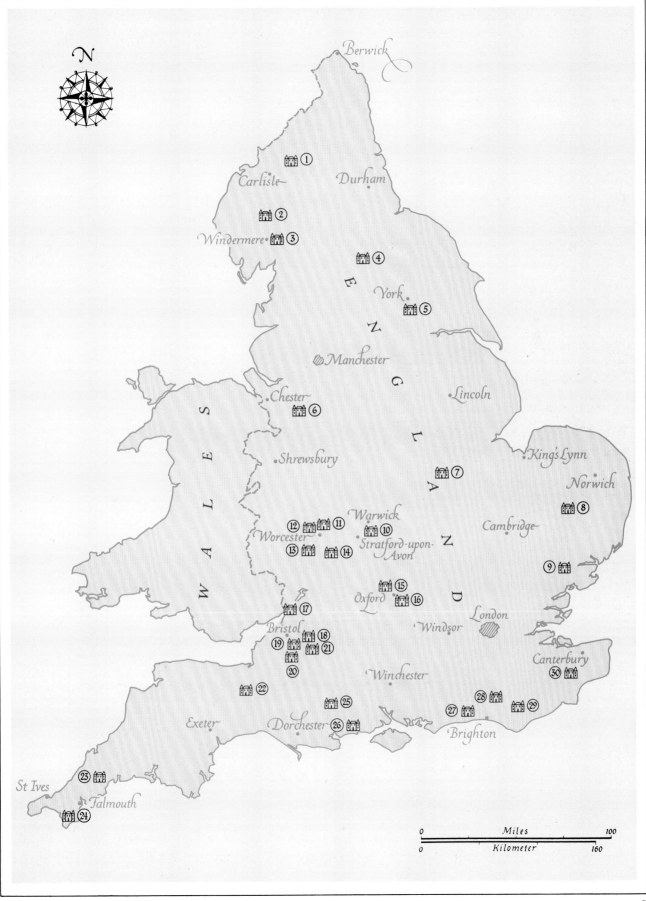

N

Berwick

Carlisle

Durham

Windermere

E N G L A N D

York

Manchester

Chester

Lincoln

W A L E S

Shrewsbury

King's Lynn

Norwich

Worcester

Warwick

Cambridge

Stratford-upon-Avon

Oxford

London

Bristol

Windsor

Canterbury

Winchester

Exeter

Dorchester

Brighton

St Ives

Falmouth

Miles

0   100

Kilometer

0   160

A warm welcome in the Scottish borderland

The countryside in the far north of England is so wild and empty that it is an agreeable surprise to come across Farlam Hall. With its smooth green lawns, neat gravel drive, and well-tended gardens, it looks like an illustration from a Jane Austen novel. Wild ducks bob about placidly on the ornamental lake in front of it, unpinioned, beguiled by regular food and kind treatment. This site has been constantly occupied for over a thousand years; the oldest part of the present building was a farmhouse in the 1600s, as documents prove. John Wesley is said to have preached at Farlam Hall, and George Stephenson's famous locomotive, The Rocket, belonged to the owners, who used it to haul coal in the local mines until it was donated to London's Science Museum.

On chilly days, a fire burns cheerfully in the grate of Farlam Hall's small front room and the owners, the Quinion family, hasten to serve you welcome refreshments beside it once you have settled in. The bedrooms are comfortable, warm, cheerful, and well-stocked with small thoughtful extras. The modest proportions of the front part of the house deceive: dinner-time reveals a vast, high-ceilinged dining room and large drawing rooms, one of which has a huge *Alice Through the Looking Glass* mirror above the mantelpiece. Décor throughout is by Mrs Quinion. The food, briskly served in a friendly manner by family members, is fresh and tasty. The chef, the Quinions' son Barry, was trained in some notable establishments. Avocado mousse with red cabbage and Solway salmon finished with cucumber and mint sauce proved as delicious as they sounded, and the desserts on the sideboard tasted as good as they looked.

Many people who stay at Farlam Hall come to see the nearby well-preserved remains of Hadrian's

Wall, built right across England by the Romans AD 117–138 to keep out marauding tribes from Scotland. Others come to fish, shoot, walk, watch birds, or merely to break their journey on the way north or south. Television and telephone are banished to a separate room each: many people are here to avoid them. Mr Quinion told me, diffidently, that guests who come for a night often stay for a week, and then return year after year. Farlam Hall is an unpretentious, comfortable, and warmly welcoming family concern.

Opposite: wild ducks on the lake outside the hotel, a sun-lit lounge, and a corner of the garden. Above: dinner is laid overlooking the lawns.

FARLAM HALL, Brampton, Nr Carlisle, Cumbria CA8 2NG. **Tel.** Hallbankgate (069 76) 234. **Telex** No. **Owners** The Quinion family. **Open** All year, *except* first 2 wks in Nov., all Feb., and Christmas. From Nov. to end Jan. closed every Mon. and Tues. **Rooms** 10 double, 1 single, all with bathrooms (2 with shower). No phone or TV in rooms. **Facilities** 3 lounges (1 with TV), bar, dining room, 4½-acre grounds, croquet. Golf nearby. **Restrictions** No children under 4 in restaurant. Dogs by prior arrangement with management only. **Terms** Moderate. Some 2-day special bargains mid-Nov. until mid-April. **Credit cards** Mastercharge/Access/Amex. **Getting there** M1, M6 to Carlisle, A69 to Brampton. Hotel is on A689 2½ miles SE of Brampton, *not* in Farlam village. About 6 hrs. **Helicopter landing** No. **Of local interest** Hadrian's Wall, Lanercost Priory ruins, Carlisle, Alston, local woollen mills. **Whole day expeditions** Follow course of Hadrian's Wall to Newcastle, thence to Durham. For Pennine scenery, follow *very* steep and winding road Alston–Penrith, with side-trip to Kirkoswald, and back via M6. Lake District. **Refreshments** Hare and Hounds, Talkin; Prospect Hill Hotel, Kirkoswald. **Dining out** Sharrow Bay Hotel, Ullswater (see p.13).

Lakeside luxury

Sharrow Bay is not so much a hotel as a legend, the forerunner of, and model for, most of England's country house hotels. Few succeed in capturing anything like its own special charm. It is the country hotel preferred by the British above all others, and it is constantly winning awards which prove this, but the owners have never become complacent. They continue to care about every crumb that leaves their kitchen, and every guest that enters their door.

In 1949 Francis Coulson bought the little gray-stone 1840s house, which has a stupendous view down Ullswater. He was joined by Brian Sack three years later. From humble beginnings as a small hotel famous for its home-made fare, Sharrow Bay has acquired a devoted staff and a varied and deliciously self-indulgent menu. Cottages and a lakeside farm now provide extra rooms. The garden has matured marvellously, and the cream bill has risen steadily into monthly thousands of pounds. Since neither owner can resist antique shops, every available corner has gradually been filled with their finds. Those who travel with much luggage should ask for a large room, because much of the storage space is already filled with board games, books, hair driers, and extra blankets – after thirty-five years you get to know what your guests might have forgotten or might want. There is a teatray with delicate china and a cookie jar, a drinks fridge, and a bathroom stacked with little extras. Everywhere is immaculate, comfortable, and snug, with heavy velvet curtains and plump soft chairs.

Dinner is splendidly formal, with waiters in stiffly starched white jackets. The choices on the menu are agonizing, since you know that all the twenty-four or so starters are equally good. Happily the next two courses are without choice. I began with tomato and tarragon soup, followed by a morsel of halibut with a fish-shaped wisp of puff pastry, and then a damson sorbet in a tall glass. The main course, a plump little Yorkshire grouse, came ringed with apple, celery, onions, bread sauce, fried breadcrumbs, allumette potatoes, redcurrant jelly, and game gravy – and that was *before* the vegetables arrived! A further impossible decision had to be made between fourteen mouth-watering desserts. I finally decided on a Regency syllabub. Coffee, cheese, and sweetmeats followed. All delectable and all prepared with an *Upstairs, Downstairs* lavish use of butter, cream, and eggs. The especially well-chosen wine-list matches the high quality of the food.

It is worth getting up early to enjoy the view down Ullswater and the smell of freshly baked croissants and brioches. The traditional British breakfast is of course superb. This is the sort of hotel that English children at boarding school, eating almost inedible food and sleeping on narrow lumpy beds, fantasize about, and that visitors from abroad, used to quantity-controlled portions, marvel at.

Opposite: a blazing fire makes the comfortable interiors even cozier. Above: one of the charming bedrooms. Overleaf: the hills surrounding Ullswater are a spectacular setting for the hotel.

SHARROW BAY COUNTRY HOUSE HOTEL, Lake Ullswater, Penrith, Cumbria CA10 2LZ. **Tel.** Pooley Bridge (085 36) 301. **Telex** No. **Owners** Francis Coulson and Brian Sack. **Open** Early March–early Dec. **Rooms** 23 double, 7 single, 4 cottage suites. 24 with tub, 2 with shower, all with phone, radio, color TV, some with tea-making facilities. **Facilities** 4 lounges, breakfast room, restaurant. 12-acre grounds and woodlands, $\frac{1}{2}$-mile lake shore with private jetty and boathouse. **Restrictions** No dogs, no children under 13. **Credit cards** No. Personal checks only. **Terms** Expensive. **Getting there** M1 (or M4, M5), then M6, Exit 40, A592 to Pooley Bridge. Hotel is about 2 miles to the s. About $5\frac{1}{2}$ hrs. **Helicopter landing** Yes (24 hrs notice). **Of local interest** Wordsworth's homes at Dove Cottage, Grasmere, and Rydal Mount, Rydal. Walking, climbing, bathing, fishing. Vale of Eden and Pennines. **Whole day expeditions** Hadrian's Wall, Penrith, tours of Lakes. **Refreshments** Pheasant, Bassenthwaite. **Dining out** Miller Howe, Windermere (see p.17).

A perfectly staged performance

John Tovey is the author of cookery books, a television personality, and a sometime theatrical entrepreneur, and his hotel, Miller Howe, has all the flair and flamboyant extravagance such a background might lead one to expect.

Perched high above Lake Windermere, in one of the most spectacular areas of the Lake District, the house is rather ordinary from the outside, but inside the reception rooms have the glamor and elegance of a Broadway stage setting. They glow with warm browns and creams, have heavy leather, brass-studded club armchairs and chesterfields, and at night look out over a floodlit garden, exotic with lush vegetation, fountains, and stone cupids. Inside are more cupids, some gilded, alcoves with dramatically lit displays of vivid blue Venetian and Bristol glass, and framed 18th-century silk embroidered panels. Vast arrangements of flowers are scattered throughout the hotel. The luxurious bedrooms are warmly centrally heated, close carpeted, and have trouser presses, hair driers, and glossy books about England thoughtfully provided. The glazed chintz matching bedcovers and curtains are tastefully patterned; bathrooms are sumptuous and have efficient showers and thick, huge towels warming on hot rails.

Dinner is An Event, for which guests are asked to assemble at 7.30, in order to discuss their choice of wines over a cocktail, and be ready to move *en masse* to the dining room on the stroke of 8.00. Once everyone is seated, the lights are lowered, and a file of young waiters whisk in the first of the many beautifully presented, interestingly flavored, and skilfully chosen courses. Daring ingredients and startling combinations are a feature of the menu, which begins always with a foreign speciality, followed by a soup,

such as parsnip and ginger with pine nuts. The next course is fish – on my visit, the halibut cooked in yoghurt, accompanied by apple, fennel, celery, and peppers with cheddar cheese, was delicious. A garnished roast, ringed with at least seven vegetables, completes the "no choice" section of the meal, in which the tastes all perfectly balance and achieve a magnificent harmony. There is a mouth-watering selection of desserts, but beware of "My Nan's tipsy trifle," since there are the stairs to climb to bed.

After a comfortable night, you are greeted as you come downstairs in the morning with a generous goblet of Buck's Fizz, compliments of Mr Tovey. As you sit down to a perfectly prepared British breakfast, the whole panorama of mountains on the far side of the lake lies before you, and you may read their names on your menu. The highly talented Mr Tovey not only creates the original and delicious meals, but also designs the striking décor. A visit to Miller Howe is a theatrical experience, perfect in every detail, and must be unique in the hotel world.

Opposite: tea is served looking over Lake Windermere. Above: a drawing room gleams with leather furniture.

MILLER HOWE, Rayrigg Road, Windermere, Cumbria LA23 1EY. **Tel.** Windermere (096 62) 2536. **Telex** No. **Owner** John Tovey. **Open** Early March–early Dec. **Rooms** 13 double, 11 with tub, 2 with shower, all with radio and casette player. TV available on request. No phones in rooms. **Facilities** 3 drawing rooms, 2 dining rooms, sun-lounge terrace, 4-acre gardens. Laundry service (Mon.–Fri.). **Restrictions** No children under 12, no dogs in public rooms. **Terms** Expensive. Some autumn and spring special terms, occasional cookery courses with all-inclusive terms. **Credit cards** Diners/Amex. **Getting there** M1, M6, Exit 36 (signposted South Lakes), A591 to Windermere until A592 turning on L, $\frac{1}{4}$ mile along road watch carefully for hotel board. About 5 hrs. **Helicopter landing** No. **Of local interest** Carlisle, Holker Hall, Levens Hall, Sizergh Castle, gardens at Lingholm, Stagshaw, Acorn Bank. Craft shops, walking, trips on Lake steamers, climbing, sailing. **Whole day expeditions** Explore high Pennine moorland country on narrow twisting A689 Brampton–Alston road and A686 Alston–Penrith road. **Refreshments** Pheasant, Bassenthwaite; Prospect Hill Hotel, nr Penrith; Howe Town, Ullswater. **Dining out** Sharrow Bay, Ullswater (see p. 13); Old Vicarage, Witherslack.

Wake to birdsong in James Herriot's Yorkshire

Jervaulx Hall has a pleasing exterior. Its graceful façade has almost Dutch gables and long stately windows. There is an elegant clock-tower on the stables to the left, a pool with a pretty dolphin fountain in the center of its circular drive, and, to the right, lawns and flower borders, a croquet lawn and huge trees, and the path that leads into the romantic ruins of Jervaulx Abbey. The Hall is probably on the site of the Abbey guest-house; it has ancient cellars and some of the walls are over two feet thick. A glass porch contains a friendly jumble of tables and chairs and a box with croquet mallets. The comfortable and homely reception hall has a wood-burning stove and many helpful books and pamphlets for those who are touring. John and Shirley Sharp, with their little Jack Russell terrier, Spot, will be waiting to welcome you.

The bedrooms are simple, with flowered wallpaper and a tea and coffee tray so that you can make yourself a hot drink. There will probably be a vase of wildflowers on the dressing table to greet you. Should you wish to telephone, there is a pay phone downstairs near the rather grand cloakroom. There is also a television in the hall, but nobody seems to bother to watch it. When you wake on a summer morning in fine weather, the birds are singing, and wild rabbits are playing on the lawn near the sundial. If you decide on a walk through the ruins, you will find wildflowers and trim paths, two huge weeping ash trees, walled courtyards and empty mullioned windows, wild roses rioting in pink and white profusion over the gray stones, and sheep grazing peacefully in the surrounding parkland.

Most guests spend the day touring the Yorkshire Dales. When I was there all the little towns were celebrating the five hundredth anniversary of the crowning of Richard III of York with as much enthusiasm as if it had happened in their lifetimes. Returning in the evening, guests will find John Sharp formally dressed in a suit waiting to take orders for

dinner. There is a modest wine-list and a choice between two dishes for each course. I enjoyed the onion and anchovy tart and the roast duckling; bowls of garden vegetables were brought round on a trolley and second helpings were encouraged. Profiteroles with chocolate sauce were followed by coffee in the drawing room, where we were joined by our host, and by Spot, as we sat and exchanged Dales gossip. The conversation could have come straight from a James Herriot novel – indeed the author himself had dined there not long before. The other guests were, like our host, from the North, and when I asked them how long it might take me to drive back to London, everyone looked blank. Nobody had bothered to drive down there for years!

Opposite: a fountain plays outside Jervaulx Hall; the abbey ruins are close by. Above: a piano invitingly open in the drawing room.

JERVAULX HALL, Jervaulx, Masham, Nr Ripon, North Yorkshire HG4 4PH. **Tel.** Bedale (0677) 60235. **Telex** No. **Owners** John and Shirley Sharp. **Open** March–Dec. **Rooms** 8 double (1 on ground floor), with bathroom and teamaking facilities. No phone or TV in rooms. **Facilities** 2 reception rooms, 1 with TV, dining room, 8-acre grounds. Fishing by arrangement. **Restrictions** None. **Terms** Moderate. **Credit cards** Visa/Access **Getting** there M1/A1, W on B6267, A6108 to Jervaulx. About 5 hrs. **Helicopter landing** Yes (2 days notice). **Of local interest** Yorkshire Dales (walking, birdwatching), Wensleydale, Richmond. **Whole day expeditions** Castle Howard, York, Harrogate, Ripon, Durham. **Refreshments** White Bear, Masham; Malt Shovel, Oswaldkirk. **Dining out** Bridge Inn, Stapleton; McCoy's Restaurant, Northallerton.

Aristocratic splendor near ancient York

Historic House Hotels is an organization which buys lovely old country houses, restores them, and opens them as luxurious country house hotels. Middlethorpe Hall, built about 1700 by a wealthy master cutler, and sometime home of the wildly eccentric traveller and diarist Lady Mary Wortley Montagu, needed months of work before it was ready to receive guests. Eight layers of paint had to be stripped from the panelling of the Oak Dining Room and parts of the magnificent woodwork of the wide staircases were expertly recarved. The black-and-white marble hall and intricate plasterwork of the ceilings took weeks to refurbish. Splendid bathrooms were installed, with the sort of solidly good-quality marble and chrome usually found only in the better European hotels. Each has an efficient shower as well as a tub. Décor was supervised by Mrs Robin Compton, whose own stately home, nearby Newby Hall, has won awards for its inspired restoration.

However, it is the quality of the welcome and care of the guests that ultimately is most important. Malcolm Broadbent, formerly of the superb Stafford Hotel in London's St James's, has brought his French wife and family to York, and is now Middlethorpe Hall's General Manager and host. Under his keen professional eye everything runs smoothly, and he is always about, greeting new arrivals, circulating in the restaurant, ready to answer enquiries or give touring advice. When I entered the elegant front hall on a cold evening, a log fire burning brightly in the hearth was instantly welcoming, and there was a liveried hall porter to carry in my luggage. My room was delightful; it had antiques, a pomander to hang among the clothes, and a supremely comfortable bed which was turned down for me at night. The walls seemed to be covered with dark plum-colored suede, but proved to have been cleverly painted.

Drinks are served in the vast drawing room, where guests can study the dinner menu and the wide-ranging wine-list, which includes some excellent vintages. The restaurant is in three adjoining rooms, where white damask cloths, polished silver, and delicate flower arrangements in fine porcelain vases complement the talented cooking of chef Aidan McCormack. Duck and orange soup, delicately flavored, turbot with wild mushrooms, freshest of fresh vegetables, a melon sorbet, and home-made truffles with coffee were all perfect.

Outside, the grounds are fast regaining their past splendor, and the ancient stable block has become especially luxurious extra bedrooms. The nearby ancient walled city of York has a history of Romans and Vikings, ghosts and legends. Its maze of narrow medieval streets encircle the towering Minster, and are packed with enticing shops and marvellous museums. Middlethorpe Hall provides the supremely comfortable base for sightseeing.

Opposite: A grand hotel both inside and out. Above: dinner is a fine display of china and silver. Overleaf: left, looking into the walled garden; right, two of the hotel's splendid interiors.

MIDDLETHORPE HALL, Bishopthorpe Road, York, North Yorkshire YO2 1QP. **Tel.** York (0904) 641241. **Telex** 57802, A/B MIDDLE G. **Owners** Historic House Hotels. General Manager, Malcolm Broadbent. **Open** All year. **Rooms** 30 (9 twin, 11 double, 3 suites, 6 single, 1 fourposter), all with tub, shower, color TV, direct-dial phone, radio. **Facilities** Hall, drawing room, library, upstairs sitting room, lift, 3 dining rooms, downstairs cellar/bar/informal restaurant, conference/dining room, laundry/dry cleaning. **Restrictions** No dogs, children under 12 at management's discretion. **Credit cards** All major cards. **Terms** Medium. **Getting there** A1, A64 to Bishopthorpe, just s of York. About 4 hrs. **Helicopter landing** Yes (same day). **Of local interest** York, Castle Howard, Beningbrough Hall, Selby. **Whole day expeditions** Newby Hall and gardens, Ripon, Fountains Abbey, Rievaulx Abbey, Shandy Hall (Coxwold). **Refreshments** Fauconberg Arms, Coxwold; Star, Harome; Ebor, Bishopthorpe. **Dining out** Pool Court, Pool-in-Wharfedale.

Gracious hospitality in a sumptuous setting

I must confess to a partiality for Rookery Hall. Appearing unannounced one Saturday for lunch, I found myself the only guest, all others having departed to some function. Instead of being waited on with glum faces by a staff who otherwise would have had a welcome rest, I was greeted with enthusiasm, served an excellent lunch, and made to feel that the one concern of the chef and his numerous assistants was that I should enjoy my meal. A subsequent stay did not disillusion me.

Rookery Hall is a vast mansion, and its grounds include a stable block, a walled garden, a lake, and parkland with ancient oak trees. Alterations by its second owner, Baron von Schröder, in the mid-1800s gave it the imposing European look it has today. Candlelight throws into relief coats-of-arms in the fine plasterwork of the ceiling of the larger dining room; the smaller has 18th-century panelling rescued from a demolished mansion. Both look out over lawns, flower borders, and a fountain to unspoilt countryside. The enormous drawing rooms, imposing staircase, and formally dressed staff could be intimidating, but are not, since everyone is friendly, courteous, and helpful. Mr and Mrs Peter Marks, who only recently became owners of this their first hotel, lived for ten years in Monte Carlo, had a holiday home in Arizona, and travelled widely. They have been able to apply their experience as guests to the organization of comfort for others. When you arrive at Rookery Hall the Marks will probably be in the hall to greet you. Staff instantly appear to carry up bags and produce a teatray with gleaming silver and china so fine it has to be handwashed. A waiting letter greets you, suggests dinner arrangements, and encourages you to ask for anything you need. Since a bowl of fruit, freshly baked cookies, high quality toiletries, and helpful touring information are already provided you are wondering what else you could possibly need when a small bottle of excellent champagne is brought up in a silver ice bucket, compliments of the management. This VIP treatment is accorded to all.

The master chef is Brian Hamilton. Dinner consisted of tiny pancakes filled with ham and gruyère in a cream sauce, a featherlight hot fish pâté, champagne sorbet, lamb with delicious vegetables, fresh local cheese, an orange-flavored crème caramel, coffee, and hand-made petits-fours. It was attentively served, perfectly seasoned, and artistically presented. The Marks are busy improving the grounds, restoring the Victorian stable block, and redecorating the traditional bedrooms. Staying at Rookery Hall is a thoroughly gracious experience.

Opposite: the hotel rises from trim lawns. Above: tea arrives in a silver service. Overleaf: left, the dining room and an exquisitely arranged salad; right, a rococo stove carries a bust of Michelangelo's "David."

ROOKERY HALL, Worleston, Nr Nantwich, Cheshire CW5 6DQ. **Tel.** Nantwich (0270) 626866. **Telex** 367169, A/B ROOKHALL. **Owners** Mr and Mrs Peter Marks. **Open** All year. **Rooms** 3 suites, 6 double, 3 single, all with bathroom, color TV, radio, and direct-dial phone. **Facilities** 2 public dining rooms, 1 private dining room, 2 salons, 28-acre grounds, tennis court, croquet, putting, coarse fishing in River Weaver, clay-pigeon shooting. **Restrictions** No children under 10, no dogs, guests are requested not to smoke during meals. **Terms** Expensive. Special breaks, special Christmas program. **Credit cards** All major cards. **Getting there** M1, M6, take Exit 16 to Audley, follow signs on A52 to Nantwich. At first roundabout take A51 to Chester. After about 2 miles take B5074 on R to Winsford. Hotel is $1\frac{1}{2}$ miles on R. About $3\frac{1}{2}$ hrs. **Helicopter landing** Yes (same day). **Of local interest** Royal Doulton, Wedgwood, and Minton potteries, Nantwich, Chester. **Whole day expeditions** Beeston Castle, Peak District. **Refreshments** Royal Oak, Worleston. **Dining out** Nothing nearby.

Designer living

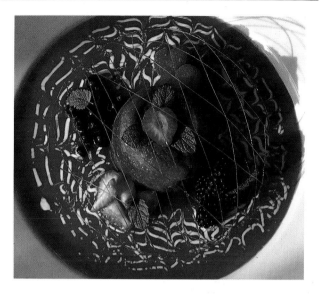

Hambleton Hall was built for house-parties. The motto above the door, "Fay ce que voudras" ("Do as you please"), reflects the philosophy of its original owner, a wealthy young bachelor. Refusing to go into the family business, he built this mansion to entertain the Prince of Wales' set – lively young people who escaped the stiff court etiquette and disapproving beady eye of Queen Victoria whenever possible. The house-party tradition continued into the 1920s; Noël Coward was staying here when he wrote *Hay Fever*.

Overlooking Rutland Water, and reached by a narrow peninsular of land that juts into the lake, Hambleton Hall has a solid Victorian stateliness. It is at the end of a curving drive, sheltered by huge cedars; terraces of flowers and shrubs lead down to parkland and the lakeside. The atmosphere of the house is one of calm sophistication. Merchant banker Tim Hart and his wife, Stefa, with the famous interior designer Nina Campbell, have created a series of beautiful and striking rooms. "Fern" is white and cool, with leafy green and dark blue touches. "Qazin" is exotically eastern, in dark red and orange, with a four-poster bed. Wallpapers, fabrics, furniture (both antique and modern), handwoven bedcovers, bedlinen, doorplates, china (individually designed for each room), and flowers are brought together in a *tour de force* of design. Jan Bos, the new General Manager, and several of his staff were formerly with London's Connaught Hotel.

Sitting in a comfortable chair by the fire, I sipped my nicely chilled dry sherry and munched miniature anchovy-filled croissants and tiny venison-pâté tartlets while studying the menu. The dining room was elegant, formal, but friendly, the food of the highest quality. A warm salad had an interesting mixture of tempting greenery with a hint of ginger and soy sauce in the dressing, sliced smoked goose breast, and pine kernels lightly roasted to bring out their flavor. A sole fillet, wrapped round a mousseline of pike, was decorated with a scarlet crayfish and a crescent of puff pastry. Roast lamb, very pink (as requested), in a dark delicious sauce was served with finely sliced potatoes and courgettes, tiny brussel sprouts, and miniature green beans. A truly wonderful dessert – cream and sweet chestnuts blended – was topped with a golden coronet of spun sugar. Succulent petits-fours accompanied excellent coffee. Upstairs, Malvern water and freshly made shortbread waited beside a neatly turned-down bed. I left feeling that I had been visiting wealthy country acquaintances with impeccable taste and perfect manners.

Opposite: the entrance bears the pleasure-lover's motto, "Do as you please." Above: a beautifully presented summer pudding. Overleaf: left, the impressive garden front and a luxurious bedroom; right, the hotel's view over Rutland Water.

HAMBLETON HALL, Hambleton, Oakham, Leicestershire, LE15 8TH. **Tel.** Oakham (0572) 56991. **Telex** 342888 A/B HAMBLE G. **Owners** Tim and Stefa Hart. General Manager, Jan Willem Bos. **Open** All year. **Rooms** 15 double, all with bathroom, color TV, radio and direct-dial phone. **Facilities** Drawing room, dining room, bar, private dining room, lift, 12-acre grounds, hard tennis court, horse riding, clay-pigeon shooting by arrangement, riding. **Restrictions** Children under 5, and dogs, by arrangement with management. **Terms** Expensive. **Credit cards** All major cards. **Getting there** A1 to Stamford, A606 direction Oakham. 1 mile before reaching Oakham, take Hambleton village turning. About 2½ hrs. **Helicopter landing** Yes (24 hrs notice). **Of local interest** Oakham, Stamford and Burghley House, Uppingham, Melton Mowbray. **Whole day expeditions** Lincoln, Boston, King's Lynn, Wisbech, Ely, Cambridge. Hotel provides helpful guidebook. **Refreshments** Fox and Hounds, Exton; Noel Arms, Langham; White Horse, Amphingham; Noel Arms, Whitwell. **Dining out** Manor House, Pickworth.

Be pampered in this cozy Victorian home

Lovers of Victoriana will be fascinated by Salisbury House. It stands primly on its gravel drive in an acre of discreetly exuberant garden, on an otherwise undistinguished road on the outskirts of Diss. Trim as a doll's house outside, inside it gleams with polished perfection. A profusion of Victorian china, prints, furniture, and "objets" jostle each other for space in the four small rooms downstairs. Upstairs are three bedrooms with brass bedsteads so tall that they must be climbed into, antique patchwork quilts, fat velvet armchairs, stripped pine tables and writing desks, and frilly swags and drapes at the windows. Bathrooms combine reassuringly modern plumbing with wooden towel horses, wicker furniture, and prints. There are thick fluffy towels, high quality bath essence and shampoo, and adequate space for clothes and luggage. Armfuls of freshly cut flowers and bowls of pot-pourri throughout the house lightly perfume the air.

The front parlor is resplendent in red plush, like a box at a Victorian theater; the back parlor has a decorative motif of dogs. The twin dining rooms, one green, one brown, display mahogany, heavy silver, cut glass, bone-handled cutlery, stuffed birds, and a striking collection of framed fans in ivory, lace, feathers, and painted silk. At the back of the house, a tall conservatory overflows with potted palms and flowering plants, and an old wash-house has been transformed into an elegant garden pavilion. Here in summer guests sit, sipping their drinks and studying their menus, while they watch the sun go down over the ruined windmill and admire the fantastical white Sebastapol geese and frillback pigeons that parade about the garden.

The food, prepared by former Michelin Guide Inspector Anthony Rudge, is interesting and varied and is served with friendly charm and deft expertise by *maître d'hôtel* Jonathan Thompson (once with the Royal Ballet). As memorable as the candlelit dinners are the breakfasts, also stylishly served, with freshly squeezed orange juice in champagne glasses, delicious croissants and breads hot from the oven, an exquisitely arranged bowl of fresh fruit, and the morning paper.

When the present owners discovered this house it was badly run down and the garden was a wilderness. They have both obviously enjoyed bringing house and garden to their present immaculate state, and delight in cosseting and indulging their fortunate guests.

Opposite: three views of this snug hotel. Above: one of the parlors, with china dogs on the mantelpiece.

SALISBURY HOUSE, 84 Victoria Road, Diss, Norfolk IP22 3JG. **Tel.** Diss (0379) 4738. **Telex** No. **Owners** Anthony Rudge and Jonathan Thompson. **Open** All year, except one week in both spring and autumn, but *closed* Sun. and Mon. every week. **Rooms** 3 double, 1 with tub, 2 with shower, all with radio and mono TV. No phones in rooms. **Facilities** 2 sitting rooms, 2 dining rooms, garden room, conservatory, garden, croquet lawn. **Restrictions** No children under 12, no dogs in public rooms (there is however a resident house dog). **Terms** Moderate. **Credit cards** No. Personal checks or cash only. **Getting there** M11/A11, A45 to Bury St Edmunds, A143 to Diss, at T junction entering Diss, turn L under railway bridge. House is just under bridge on L. About 2 hrs. **Helicopter landing** No. **Local interest** Bury St Edmunds, Wingfield College (with music festival), Norwich, Sainsbury art center at University of East Anglia. **Whole day expeditions** Newmarket, Cambridge, Ely. East coast: Aldeburgh (June music festival), Southwold, Orford. Framlingham, King's Lynn, Houghton Hall, Sandringham House (home of H.M. The Queen), Walsingham, and Holkham Hall. **Refreshments** King's Head, Orford; Adam and Eve, Norwich. **Dining out** Angel, Bury St Edmunds; Shipdham Place, Shipdham.

Live in style in Constable country

Much favored by film stars and diplomats passing through London, Maison Talbooth is in the heart of the gentle countryside made famous in the early 19th century by the paintings of John Constable and surprisingly unchanged since.

The plain, color-washed exterior of the Maison Talbooth gives no hint of the opulence of its large, luxurious bedrooms, lavishly draped and individually furnished, which are named for English Romantic poets. Each has an ornate bed or beds, an elaborate bathroom – two with a large sunken round tub on a raised dais – plenty of cupboard space, direct-dial telephone, color television, a mini bar, and comfortable chairs and settees. There is no impression of staying in a hotel. You arrive, sign the guest book, the friendly and helpful staff settle you into your room, offer refreshments and vanish. You may then wander at will in the 2-acre grounds or relax in the spacious drawing room, or in the comfort of your bedroom, undisturbed. You have only, however, to lift a telephone for instant service.

Breakfast arrives in your room in the morning, elegantly presented: there is no restaurant at the Maison Talbooth. Owner Gerald Milsom has however provided his guests with a wide choice of different menus close at hand. Le Talbooth, a lovely old timbered building painted by Constable, is half-a-mile away on the River Stour. It serves classical French and English dishes in a formal setting and has an excellent and skilfully chosen wine-list. The Dedham Vale Hotel, by contrast, has a delightful, yellow-draped, plant-hung, Edwardian-style conservatory restaurant, with a menu designed to tempt the transatlantic customer and a pleasingly unBritish willingness to serve large cups of coffee *with* dessert,

if required. Totally and unashamedly American is the menu at The Pier fish restaurant, the fourth Milsom establishment, half-an-hour away by car at the deepwater port of Harwich. The big Scandinavia-bound ferries pass startlingly close to its windows, but no longer tie up alongside as in Victorian times, when Harwich was the Great Eastern railway terminus.

East Anglia is a much underrated part of England. Its churches, huge and elegant, dwarf the little villages huddling round them and were built with the wealth of the medieval wool trade. Look up into the darkness of their lofty wooden rafters: the beam ends often carry flights of serene angels with outstretched gilded wings.

Throughout his establishments, Mr Milsom – a frequent visitor to the USA – has revitalized old English ways with New World ideas. He provides a comfortable and efficient base for touring the area, and a delightful rural retreat from busy London.

Opposite: a Constable-like view of the Dedham Vale Hotel.
Above: a sumptuous bathroom in Maison Talbooth. Overleaf: left, a spectacular display of food in the Dedham Vale Hotel; right, the half-timbered façade of the restaurant Le Talbooth and one of Maison Talbooth's impressive bedrooms.

MAISON TALBOOTH, Stratford Road, Dedham, Colchester, Essex CO7 6HN. **Tel.** Colchester (0206) 322367. **Telex** No. DEDHAM VALE HOTEL, Stratford Road, Dedham, Colchester, Essex CO7 6HW. **Tel.** (0206) 322273. **Telex** No. **Owner** Gerald Milsom. **Open** All year. **Rooms** *Maison Talbooth*: 1 suite, 9 double, all with bathroom (9 with tub, 1 with shower), all with color TV, phone, private bar. Radio on request. 5 rooms on ground floor, baby listening. *Dedham Vale Hotel*: 1 suite, 5 double, all with bathroom, radio, color TV, phone. **Facilities** *Maison Talbooth*: Large hall/drawing room, 2-acre grounds. *Dedham Vale Hotel*: Lounge, bar, restaurant, 3-acre grounds, 100 yards from river. **Restrictions** No dogs.

Terms Medium. **Credit cards** All major cards. **Getting there** A12, turning off NE of Colchester at Stratford St Mary. About 1¼ hrs. **Helicopter landing** Yes (same day). **Of local interest** Constable country, Flatford Mill, villages of Kersey and Nayland, half-timbered market town of Lavenham. Long Melford, Colchester. **Whole day expeditions** Cambridge, Newmarket, Bury St Edmunds, Ely, Norwich. **Refreshments** Woolpack, and Fleece, Coggeshall; Marlborough Head, Dedham; House without a Name, Easthorpe; Fort St George, Cambridge. Olde Ferry Boat (with ghost), Holywell, nr Cambridge. **Dining out** Bear, Nayland.

1920s elegance in a glorious garden

When Jeremy Mort, who already had hotel experience, and Allan Holland, successful entrepreneur and inspired, self-taught gourmet cook, first saw Mallory Court, a twenties mansion in its own ten-acre estate, they knew at once that this was the somewhere special they had been looking for. Although the house had always been a family home, they firmly believed that a building designed for a gracious life-style and frequent house parties must work marvellously as a hotel. Without feasibility studies or market research, they plunged into the mammoth task of restoring the neglected rooms and overgrown gardens of this lovely country estate to their original glory. First, they refurbished the front part of the house, and opened it as a restaurant. The delicious food produced by Allan, working initially in somewhat primitive conditions in the original kitchen, and the delightful and attentive service supervised by Jeremy in the oak-panelled dining room with its cool green linen napery, proved an instant success. They were then able, room by room, to restore the fine woodwork, original bathrooms, spacious reception rooms, and large bedrooms. Finally they turned their attention to the terraces, rose garden, water garden, squash court, swimming pool, and orchard. When they added anything, such as extra bathrooms, they used fittings of the same high quality as the originals.

Mallory Court is now immaculate. The lovingly tended, exquisitely orderly gardens are glowing with color. Inside the house, everything is polished and shining, and the staff are delighted to see you when you arrive. Bedrooms and bathrooms are provided with every thoughtful detail. The one suite has not only a large balcony overlooking garden and beautiful countryside, but also an enormous bathroom with two bathtubs and a tall, free-standing, plate-glass shower stall. The cosseted guests, having relaxed with television or one of the many interesting books, and thumbed through the comprehensive touring information provided, come down to comfortable chairs, freshly-baked small delicacies served with pre-dinner drinks, and the contemplation of a tempting menu. I tried the crustacean consommé (light and appetizing), asparagus in featherlight pastry with a slightly orange-flavored hollandaise (different and nice), quail with fresh grapes (juicy and tender), and a perfect raspberry soufflé. Hand-made chocolates followed with the coffee; the wine-list was of high quality. The whole atmosphere was peaceful and relaxing. The personality of the owners does not intrude: Jeremy Mort is almost always there, but is quiet and self-effacing. All I saw of Allan Holland was his tall white chef's hat and starched jacket gleaming in the distance as he gathered herbs and garnishings in the early morning from the superb kitchen garden. Mallory Court is a place to which my thoughts, when I am busy, bothered, or harrassed, turn longingly back.

Opposite: Coffee in an elegant setting. Above: a welcoming bedroom. Overleaf: left, the hotel at night; right, a view of the gardens and a glimpse into one of the stylish bathrooms.

MALLORY COURT, Harbury Lane, Tachbrook Mallory, Nr Bishops Tachbrook, Leamington Spa, Warwickshire CV33 9QB. **Tel.** Leamington Spa (0926) 30214. **Telex** 317294 A/B MALORY G. **Owners** Jeremy Mort and Allan Holland. **Open** All year except for the 3 weeks after 25 Dec. **Rooms** 1 suite, 7 double, 1 single, all with bathroom, phone, radio, color TV. 1 with four-poster bed. **Facilities** Lounge, drawing room, dining room, sun lounge, 10-acre grounds, water garden, rose garden, terraces, outdoor swimming pool, squash courts, croquet, golf 2 miles away. **Restrictions** No children under 12, no dogs. **Terms** Medium. **Credit cards** Access/Euro/Amex/Visa. **Getting there** M1, at Exit 16, A45 W, into A425 to Leamington Spa. Take A452 from Leamington Spa; after 2 miles, turn L towards Harbury. Hotel about 100 yards on R. About 2½ hrs. **Helicopter landing** Yes (24 hrs notice). **Of local interest** Royal Leamington Spa, Stratford-upon-Avon, Warwick, north Cotswolds. **Whole day expeditions** Oxford, Gloucester, Cheltenham. **Refreshments** King's Head, Wellesbourne; Holly Bush, Priors Marston. **Eating out** Grafton Manor, Bromsgrove (see p.43); Hills, Stratford-upon-Avon.

A family home rich in historic associations

Those who wish a hotel to be either very grand or very informal may be confused by Grafton Manor, since the house itself, its setting, the restaurant, and the food, are grand, but the track leading to it, and the owners – the delightful Morris family – are informal. The Manor is noted in the Doomsday Book as belonging to a nephew of William the Conqueror; the present house was erected in 1567 as the principal seat of the Earls of Shrewsbury, though part was rebuilt after a disastrous fire in the 1700s. Conspirators in the Gunpowder Plot of 1605 are known to have stayed here before leaving for their ill-fated mission in London. They probably met upstairs in the Great Parlor, with its vast crested overmantle, which together with the huge entrance porch survived the fire untouched. In the evenings, drinks and exceptionally delicious canapés are served here. The restaurant, awarded three red crossed knives and forks and a red M from Michelin – high praise indeed – is downstairs. Carrot and coriander soup was served in a large tureen which was left on the table for further sampling; the bread was warm and home-made. A sea- and shell-fish soufflé flan was light and delicate, trimmed with a sprig of chervil and fennel and a purple borage flower. A complete tiny pigeon-pudding had a rich sauce and an accompaniment of perfect vegetables. Home-made sorbets, hand-made chocolates, and excellent coffee completed a perfectly seasoned, delectable meal. The wine-list is notable for some exceptional Burgundies. I retired to sit luxuriously before the twirly cast-iron grate of the gas coal fire in my bedroom.

The family themselves (father, mother, daughter, and two sons), and not a decorator, have restored the bedrooms one by one with ingenuity and charm, making light-fittings, hunting out large-patterned papers to suit the high-ceilinged rooms, and choosing rich fabrics which have been expertly sewn by a local lady. Bathrooms are luxurious. Outside is a giant herb garden (once a cricket pitch), divided into big squares. The house has its own chapel, tithe barn and a big walled garden which the Morrises hope to restore. There is a medieval "fish stew," or holding-pond, for fish from the two-acre lake, and an ancient ruined dovecot whose fate is alas uncertain, given the investment required to restore its full splendor. There is a distant prospect of the motorway. If you arrive early, you may surprise the family in sneakers and jeans, or indeed have to hunt about to find them. But they are so welcoming you feel like a relative coming home – which is, after all, how a family-run hotel should feel.

Opposite: the red-brick exterior is dominated by the 16th-century porch. Below: the food is as elegantly arranged as the checkerboard herb garden. Above: one of the comfortable bedrooms.

GRAFTON MANOR, Grafton Lane, Bromsgrove, Hereford and Worcester B61 7HA. **Tel.** Bromsgrove (0527) 31525 or 37247. **Telex** No. **Owner** John and June Morris. **Open** All year. **Rooms** 4 double, 1 suite (more in preparation), all with bathroom (2 have wall shower), color TV, direct-dial phone. **Facilities** Great Parlor, 2 restaurants, 25-acre grounds, 2-acre lake with coarse fishing. **Restrictions** No children under 5, no dogs. **Terms** Medium. **Credit cards** All major cards. **Getting there** M1, M6 round Birmingham. Take M5 s. Off at Exit 4, through Bromsgrove, take A38 towards Worcester. About 1 mile after Bromsgrove watch carefully for Grafton Lane on R. About 3 hrs. **Helicopter landing** No. **Of local interest** Avoncroft Museum of Buildings, Worcester, Royal Brierly crystal factory, Stratford-upon-Avon, Warwick. **Whole day expeditions** Welsh border castles, Ludlow, north Cotswolds. **Refreshments** Eagle and Sun, Droitwich; Galton Arms, Tiverton. **Dining out** Mallory Court, Bishops Tachbrook (see p.39); Browns, Worcester; Jonathan's, Oldbury.

Traditional luxury in a hotel overlooking the Welsh hills

It seems a shame that the traveller should so often speed up the motorways to the big industrial cities of the Midlands, and on to the Lakes and the North, without stopping to explore some of the lovely old black-and-white-timbered towns of the counties bordering Wales. Their names – Gloucester, Worcester, Hereford – read like a cast-list of dukes from a Shakespeare history play. Their cathedrals and market squares, inns and streets were ancient when Shakespeare was born; many still stand.

For anybody looking for a comfortable base from which to tour the area, The Elms, a handsome Queen Anne house of 1710, has a solidly traditional atmosphere reminiscent of pre-war luxury trains and liners. There is always a boy in a neat green jacket to carry up your bags, an efficient barman in the Library Bar to mix your favorite drink, a well-trained waiter in the sedate dining room, where tables are pleasantly spaced so that you are not obliged to share your neighbor's conversation and where an excellent classical guitarist plays softly during dinner by candlelight. The Elms has been lucky to escape the attentions of a fashionable designer. The rooms are not only individual and pleasant, with country house touches like bowls of fruit, fresh flowers, books, and touring information, but also have practical bathrooms designed by professionals and rapid room service. The gardens are glorious, with shaven lawns, bright flower borders, trim hedges, and views stretching to the misty blue Welsh hills.

Though recently acquired by a self-effacing Canadian gentleman, the hotel remains unflashily and reassuringly British. The management is still

under the keen but benevolent eye of Rita Mooney, now entering her second decade with the hotel. The new young English chef, Nigel Lambert, is rapidly establishing a wide reputation. His spinach soufflé with anchovy sauce was a subtle balance of flavors, his mango sorbet perfectly judged to clear the palate and not too sweet, his Dover sole was grilled to juicy perfection and accompanied by potatoes with a hint of cheese, carrots so fresh that they really tasted like carrots, and firm beans. I finished with a perfect apple charlotte from the exciting dessert trolley. The selection of cheese is very good and a broad range of luxury wines includes some excellent clarets.

As well as tours to local pottery and china factories, visits can be arranged to stately homes nearby, which include the opportunity to meet and sometimes to dine with their owners. The staff are never too busy to stop and answer questions or help to plan trips: The Elms is both caring and professional.

Opposite: the gracious building contains splendid rooms enriched with antiques. Above: looking through a window to the Welsh hills in the hazy distance.

THE ELMS HOTEL, Abberley, Nr Worcester, Hereford and Worcester WRT6 6AT. **Tel.** Great Witley (029921) 666. **Telex** 337105 A/B ELMS G. **Owner** Celebrated Country Hotels. General Manager, Rita Mooney. **Open** All year. **Rooms** 23 double, 2 single, 2 suites, all with bathroom, color TV, direct-dial phone, trouser press, etc. 9 rooms are in stable annex. **Facilities** Hall, Blue Room, Gallery Room, Library Bar, dining room, and a private conference/dining room. 13-acre grounds, putting green, croquet, hard tennis court. **Restrictions** No dogs. **Terms** Moderate. Special breaks and Christmas programs. **Credit cards** All major cards. **Getting there** M40 to Oxford, A40 to Cheltenham to join M5 north. At Exit 6 take A449 N, turn L on to A443 after $5\frac{1}{2}$ miles. Abberley signposted R after 9 miles. About 3 hrs. **Of local interest** Golf and horse racing nearby. Cathedral and china factory at Worcester, Elgar's Birthplace Museum (Broadheath). **Whole day expeditions** Cotswolds, Stratford-upon-Avon, Malvern Hills, Hereford. **Refreshments** Peacock, Tenby Wells; Hundred House, Abberley. **Dining out** Venture Inn, Ombersley; Browns, Worcester.

A tranquil rural retreat

The name "Hope End" does not signify despair, but has the old English local meaning "a place at the end of a hidden valley," which exactly describes this unique house. The huge estate surrounding it, in the lovely Malvern Hills, was owned by Elizabeth Barrett Browning's father in the early 1800s. He built for his wife and eleven children a vast Moorish extravaganza of a house with minarets, extending (and dwarfing) the original modest Queen Anne building. It was Elizabeth's home for twenty-three years of her early life, before the family moved to Wimpole Street in London – from which she eloped with poet Robert Browning. A later owner demolished much of the fantastic structure, leaving just one lone minaret, a huge archway, iron gates, some stables, and the little red-brick Queen Anne house. These were inherited by Patricia Hegarty, a teacher. With her lawyer husband, John, she has transformed them into a most intriguing family home and country hotel.

The Hegartys are serious but kind and their delightful house is immaculate. Natural wood, sealed but not painted, is used everywhere, even in bathrooms. There are two enormous black wood-burning stoves to sit round in the evenings although the house itself is beautifully warm. There are books everywhere, but no television and only one pay phone. The peace of the valley, the enormous trees, the grassy slopes leading down to a lake largely taken over by bullrushes and wild mallards, the smell of wood smoke, the neatness and harmony of colors in the house, and the faint aroma of delicious food in the making reminded me of a New England house deep in the woods or a Swiss mountain cabin. One bedroom is in a cottage totally removed from the house, surrounded by trees, birds, and rabbits, and evokes delight – or alarm – at its solitude.

Patricia Hegarty cooks only locally produced meat, fish, and game, and uses fruit from her own trees, vegetables from her own walled kitchen garden. The lentil soup had smoky overtones from good ham stock, the brown bread was freshly baked and the lamb was accompanied by vegetables picked just before cooking. It was followed by a mixed salad, fresh local cheese, an egg custard with a swirl of caramel and heavy cream, and a selection of either coffee or exotic teas. The good wine-list has a wide range of half-bottles. There is no choice on the menu, but it changes for every meal. Pure Malvern water – so thoughtfully provided in bottles by many hotels – here is on tap from springs in the local hills.

House martins nest under the eaves; bantams wander in the yard; rural, tranquil, and quietly excellent, this is every city-dweller's dream of escape.

Opposite: a peaceful country setting – and a minaret! Below is a beautiful display of the local produce that goes into Patricia Hegarty's cooking. Above: one of the harmoniously decorated rooms.

HOPE END COUNTRY HOUSE HOTEL, Hope End, Ledbury, Hereford and Worcester HR8 1DS. **Tel.** Ledbury (0531) 3613. **Telex** No. **Owners** John and Patricia Hegarty. **Open** Last weekend in Feb. to last weekend in Nov. **Rooms** 5 twin in house, 1 double under minaret across courtyard, 1 double in cottage, all with bathroom. *No* TV, radio, or phone in bedrooms. **Facilities** 2 sitting rooms, 1 dining room, 40-acre grounds including parkland, bluebell woods, lake, etc. Walled garden. **Restrictions** No dogs, no children, no smoking in dining room. **Terms** Moderate. Dinner incl.; reductions for longer stays. **Credit cards** All major cards. **Getting there** M40/A40 to Cheltenham via Oxford. M5 to Exit 9 (Tewkesbury), A438 to Ledbury, B4214 under railway bridge, turn R to Wellington Heath, after about 2 miles bear R. Hotel on L. About 2½ hrs. **Helicopter landing** No. **Of local interest** Malvern Hills and Three Choirs music festival (August), walks, gardens. Tewkesbury. **Whole day expeditions** Cheltenham, Gloucester, Hay-on-Wye (book shops), Wye Valley, Border castles, Offa's Dyke (footpath), Welsh mountains. **Refreshments** Cottage of Content, Carey; Fleece, Bretforton; Rhydspence, Whitney on Wye; Butcher's Arms, Woolhope. **Dining out** Crôque-en-Bouche, Malvern; Walnut Tree, Abergavenny. (NB terms at Hope End include dinner.) Bookings of 2 or more nights preferred.

Cotswold comforts in a medieval manor

Buckland Manor is exactly what comes to mind if one imagines an ancient manor house in the Cotswolds: a rambling, picturesque, honey-colored stone building close by the tower of the village church. Buckland is an enchanting place, secluded and quiet, although only two miles from the famously beautiful village of Broadway, with its many craft and antique shops but, alas, over-plentiful summer visitors.

Adrienne and Barry Berman found the 13th-century Manor in excellent condition when in 1982 they created a comfortable hotel from what until then had always been a private house, without loss of atmosphere or charm. The bedrooms have soft, fitted carpets, direct-dial telephones and color televisions; all have exceptionally luxurious bathrooms – some also have excellent showers (so rare in England). There is a gracious dining room, hung with historic portraits in oils, which has pleasant country views by day and at night is softly lit by many candles. It was added to the Manor at the beginning of this century, when many of the rooms were panelled in dark oak.

This is a place in which to relax and be pampered. The Bermans are most anxious that their guests should enjoy their stay, and spare no pains to ensure their comfort. There is a subtle chef, Robert Elsmore, as excellent as any to be found in London, and an *à la carte* menu, a relief after the set menus of many country house hotels. I found their home-smoked breast of wild duck, served on mange-tout peas with a truffle sauce, and poached fillet of Dover sole stuffed with a marvellously delicate seafood mousse absolutely delicious, though I queried the rather modest size of the portions with the chef. He is a large man, but judges portions by his own moderate appetite, so for the especially hungry I would suggest the soup, which is brought to the table in a large tureen and left there for guests to dip into at will, the excellent and plentiful home-baked bread, and the desserts, which are elaborate, delicious, and generous. I was impressed by the splendid and imaginative wine-list. The petits-fours which arrive with the coffee are hand-made and memorable.

Behind the Manor, well tended gardens rise up the hillside to a series of terraces, with rose beds, arbors, and walks. Beyond is a little stream bordered by water-loving plants and an uncultivated area where wild orchids and snake's-head fritillaries grow.

Buckland Manor is quiet and rural, yet luxurious and sophisticated, and is ideally placed for exploring the many delights of the Cotswolds, for visiting Stratford-upon-Avon or Cheltenham, or for pausing en route to Scotland or the north of England.

Opposite: roses in bloom in the well-kept gardens. Above: four-poster comfort. Overleaf: luxury, superb food, and a glorious Cotswolds setting.

BUCKLAND MANOR, Buckland, Nr Broadway, Gloucestershire WR12 7LY. **Tel.** Broadway (0386) 852626. **Telex** No. **Owners** Barry and Adrienne Berman. **Open** All year. **Rooms** 11 double, all with bathroom, 3 have shower as well as tub. Direct-dial phones, color TV, radio on request. 2 four-poster beds, some ground-floor rooms. **Facilities** 2 sitting-rooms, writing room, dining room, 10-acre grounds, gardens, heated pool, tennis court, putting green. **Restrictions** No children under 12; dogs in kennels only. **Terms** Medium. Some winter and special event all-inclusive terms. **Credit cards** All major cards. **Getting there** M40 to Oxford, A40 to Burford, A424 to Broadway via Stow-on-the-Wold. In Broadway L on A46 (signposted Cheltenham), L again after 1½ miles (signposted Buckland). 1½–2 hrs. **Helicopter landing** Yes (24 hrs notice). **Of local interest** Cheltenham, Stratford-upon-Avon. Cotswolds market towns (Cirencester, Chipping Campden, Stow) and many exquisite villages. Antique and local crafts shops, riding, golf. Gardens at Hidcote, Kiftsgate, Barnsley House. **Whole day expeditions** Oxford, Woodstock, Broughton Castle. **Refreshments** Old Bull, Inkeberrow; Fox and Hounds, Great Wolford. **Dining out** Mallory Court, Bishops Tachbrook (see p.39).

Home is a castle with royal connections

Thornbury is everything that a castle should be. It has battlements and towers looking towards the Welsh hills. There are turrets and tall twisting Tudor brick chimneys and inscribed on its gatehouse and overmantles are the coat of arms and badges of the ancestors of the Dukes of Buckingham. Henry VIII spent ten of his thousand days with Anne Boleyn here, and Mary Tudor lived here for some years before becoming queen. Kenneth Bell, the present owner, still seems amazed that he should possess such a piece of history, but it is thanks to him that it is today in magnificent condition. Twenty years ago he opened part of the castle as a restaurant. Since then he has worked steadily on the building and its grounds, re-creating a lovely garden within the outer walls, planting a vineyard in the ancient base-court, where in former times castle retainers and livestock lived, and most recently refurbishing the bedrooms to become a hotel.

You might imagine that it would be impossible to make a castle comfortable, but that is what Mr Bell has done. Corridors are carpeted and well-lit. Bedrooms have high ceilings and tall mullioned windows with warmly lined curtains, plenty of space for clothes and luggage, thoroughly modern bathrooms, many extra small luxuries, and, in several cases, impressive four-poster beds. The main suites are stupendous: the upper room in the octagonal tower has an almost oriental canopy of deep rose brocade over its four-poster, an open hearth, and a bathroom with gold-plated fittings. Before dinner guests study the menu and magnificent wine-list in the Old Library, which looks out over the clipped yew hedges and flower borders to the tower of the village church beyond. Sorrel soup, venison and cherry pie in its own little dish with a perfect crust, delicious fresh vegetables, and damson icecream were

excellent, well presented, and charmingly served by staff who are as international as the clientèle.

Kenneth Bell, not content with producing his own wine, has many future projects in mind: to reclaim the medieval tiled floor of the vanished great banqueting hall; to train and fly falcons; to reconstruct the portcullis. He even has two wild boar, from which he is hoping to breed for the table, but they are not being very co-operative, so any wild boar pâté on the menu will not for the moment be home produced!

Opposite: heraldic glass in the dining room. Above: garden chairs under the battlements. Overleaf: the atmosphere of a medieval castle lingers on – although Henry VIII never slept in so comfortable a four-poster!

THORNBURY CASTLE, Thornbury, Bristol, Avon BS12 1HH. **Tel.** Thornbury (0454) 412647 and 418511. **Telex** 449986 A/B CASTLE G. **Owner** Kenneth Bell. **Open** All year, except 5 days at Christmas. **Rooms** 3 suites, 7 doubles, 2 singles. All with bathroom, color TV, radio, phone. **Facilities** Overnight guests' lounge, reception hall, 2 dining rooms, 15-acre grounds with vineyard. **Restrictions** No dogs, no children under 12. **Terms** Expensive. **Credit cards** All major cards. **Getting there** Take M4 to Exit 20. On to A38 N. After 4 miles, turn L onto B4061 for Thornbury. About $2\frac{1}{2}$ hrs. **Helicopter landing** Yes (24 hrs notice). **Of local interest** Thornbury village, Berkeley Castle, Bristol. Golf by arrangement. **Whole day expeditions** Wye Valley, Cotswolds, Gloucester, Cheltenham, Bath. **Refreshments** Anchor, Oldbury. **Dining out** Harvey's, Bristol; Gentle Gardener, Tetbury.

In the heart of Georgian Bath

Bath is England's most elegant town and The Hole in the Wall is a delightful Georgian house in the middle of the historic center, facing down the main shopping street. A few steps away from the best of the antique shops and close to the museums, the Abbey, the Roman baths, the theater, parks, terraces, and river, its only problem is parking – car drivers should consult the owners when booking. The traffic in an ancient city like Bath is highly confusing and I always get lost in the one-way system, no matter how often I go there. Those visitors not in the first flush of youth should note that the whole city is built on steep hillsides and that the hotel is on several floors, linked by a precipitous staircase.

The owners, Sue and Tim Cumming, are friendly, quiet people, always helpful, who trained with George Perry-Smith of The Riverside in Cornwall (see page 79). They are puzzled when they are asked whether they accept children in their hotel. "Who," they ask, "could possibly not welcome children?" Their down-to-earth approach to life is evident in the unpretentious way in which their superb French-Provincial-inspired food is presented in the simple but charming basement restaurant that was once a Georgian coal-hole and kitchen. It has whitewashed walls, and uncluttered polished tables. There is the faint, delicious perfume of fresh herbs, warm bread, and good things bubbling on the stove that identifies the good restaurant just as surely as the depressing smell of rancid fat and stale alcohol seems to haunt a bad one. Their spinach and watercress soup, venison and fruit pie, inspired and varied cold table, and home-made sorbets and icecreams are famous throughout England. The wine-list has interesting clarets, excellent Burgundies, and a wide range of Rhine and Loire wines, all reasonably priced.

Breakfast is served in a modern room upstairs, with croissants straight from the oven, home-made jams and marmalades, and delicious coffee. Tables are well spaced, nobody hurries you over your morning paper, the dining chairs are padded and comfortable, and on a fine day the morning sun streams in through the window.

The simple bedrooms have good beds, antiques, and several have a view out over an intriguing jumble of roofs and chimneypots. The bathrooms are often vast and self-indulgent, with tiles specially hand-painted for the Cummings by an artist friend. The public areas in the hotel have plenty of inviting easy chairs, books, magazines (including marvellous old bound copies of *Punch*), and fresh flowers. This is not a glossy hotel. Those wishing to be pampered would probably prefer one of the grander establishments in the countryside near Bath. But, like its owners, it is relaxed, civilized, and straightforward.

Opposite: the cool and charming cellar restaurant. Above: hand-painted tiles in the bathroom and a view of rooftops.

THE HOLE IN THE WALL, 16 George Street, Bath, Avon BA1 2EN. **Tel.** Bath (0225) 25243. **Telex** No. **Owners** Tim and Sue Cumming. **Open** All year. **Rooms** 8 double, all with bathroom (tub and shower), phone, radio, color TV, tea-making and baby-listening facilities. **Facilities** Reception area, 2 lounges, 2 bars, 2 dining rooms. **Restrictions** No pets. **Terms** Moderate. **Credit cards** All major cards. **Getting there** M4, turn off for Bath at Exit 18 (A46). About 2 hrs. **Helicopter landing** No. **Of local interest** In Bath itself, Roman Baths, Costume Museum, American Museum, Carriage Museum, Museum of Bookbinding, Abbey, Theatre Royal. Of the many splendid Georgian streets, be sure not to miss the Royal Crescent, the Circus, or Queen's Square. **Whole day expeditions** Bristol, Wells, Mendip Hills, Cheddar Gorge, gardens at Stourhead and Bowood, country houses at Dyrham, Longleat, and Lacock. **Refreshments** White Hart, Ford; Red Lion, Lacock. **Dining out** Homewood Park, Hinton Charterhouse (see p. 73); Hunstrete House, Hunstrete (see p. 65).

A centuries-old tradition of hospitality

The village of Hunstrete (once "Houndstreet") is first mentioned in AD 936. Hunstrete House itself was built in the 18th century, of golden stone which time has weathered to gray. A square, stately building, in wooded grounds, approached up a long drive that curves gently through the deer park, it is at first sight so imposing as to be slightly intimidating. This impression is quickly dispelled by the friendly warmth of the greeting by the staff. The comfortable chairs, huge arrangements of flowers from the garden, magazines and books scattered about, and the fires which are rapidly kindled in the many fireplaces if the day turns chilly, evoke an atmosphere of home rather than hotel. The owner, John Dupays, supervises the care of the magnificent gardens, and his wife, Thea, has collected the many antiques and chosen the lovely fabrics that make each of the large, well-furnished bedrooms individual and charming. Each bedroom is named after a native British bird, with a framed print of that bird on the wall: I was intrigued to find myself staying in "Pipit." Seven of the rooms are in a converted stable block, which is reached by crossing a charming courtyard almost Mediterranean in atmosphere, with a fountain and many cheerful flowers. The rooms in the annexe are as spacious and luxurious as those in the main building.

The standard of the cooking matches the comfort of the house. The food is elegantly served in the attractive pink dining rooms, which have a view of manicured lawns and colorful flowerbeds. The chef concentrates on ingredients of outstanding quality cooked to perfection, with fine sauces and delicious vegetables, rather than endless mixtures of unlikely tastes combined more for novelty than for the pleasure of the diner. There is a wide choice of dishes, including, when I stayed, roast beef, lamb, Dover sole, and Scottish salmon. Fish is cooked superbly, pastry is light and feathery, the lamb pink and juicy, and the vegetables crisp but not crunchy. Desserts are especially memorable – for instance, a choux pastry swan filled with a light chocolate cream and surrounded by a tangy orange sauce. Hand-made chocolates and sweetmeats accompany the coffee. It must be pointed out, I feel, that the venison on the menu comes from Scotland, and not from the deer grazing around the house! The broad-based wine-list features some exceptional wines and is compiled with evident expertise.

The welcoming hospitality offered to guests at Hunstrete House maintains a long tradition stretching back to medieval times, when a monastery stood on the site and entertained weary pilgrims on their way to the miraculous shrine at Glastonbury Abbey.

Opposite and above: gray walls and glowing interiors make an intriguing contrast. Overleaf: left, sun catches the fountain's horses; right, warmth and style are combined in the rooms.

HUNSTRETE HOUSE, Hunstrete, Chelwood, Nr Bristol, Avon BS19 4NS. **Tel.** Compton Dando (076 18) 578. **Telex** 449540 A/B HUNHSE. **Owners** John and Thea Dupays. **Open** All year, except early Jan. **Rooms** 2 suites, 15 doubles, 3 singles. All with bathroom, phone, radio, color TV. 7 of these rooms are in an annex (4 on ground floor). Hand, not wall, showers. **Facilities** Drawing room, library, bar, 2 dining rooms, 90-acre grounds, heated outdoor swimming pool, hard tennis court, croquet lawn, coarse fishing. **Restrictions** No children under 9; no dogs. **Terms** Medium. **Credit cards** Visa/Amex. **Getting there** M4, A46 to Bath, then A368; the hotel is 8 miles SW of Bath. About 2½–3 hrs. **Helicopter landing** Yes (2 days notice). **Of local interest** Bath, Bristol, Wells, Berkeley Castle, Peter Scott's Wildfowl Trust at Slimbridge, Cheddar Gorge, Glastonbury, Lacock village, Bowood Gardens. **Whole day expeditions** Over Severn Bridge into Wales, to Chepstow and Wye Valley; S to Dorset and Thomas Hardy country; SW to Devon, Exmoor and Doone Valley. **Refreshments** White Hart, Ford; Red Lion, Lacock; Rifleman's Arms, Glastonbury. **Dining out** Hole in the Wall, Bath (see p. 63); Homewood Park, Hinton Charterhouse (see p. 73); Thornbury Castle, Thornbury (see p. 59).

In the grand style

What do you do when you inherit from your family many very beautiful, very large, very much loved pieces of 18th-century furniture? The answer, in the case of Peter and Christine Smedley, is that you buy a magnificent 18th-century mansion from the editor of the London *Times*, restore it to its original palatial grandeur, using the best materials and finest craftsmanship, add marble bathrooms and warm central heating, an elegant restaurant, and a staff of friendly local girls in neat uniforms, and open it as a superb country hotel.

Ston Easton is also the Smedleys' home, complete with an amiable spaniel and family portraits in the yellow dining room. Each room is individually charming: the lofty Palladian Saloon; the panelled restaurant in the Tudor core of the house; the enormous bedrooms with lofty four-posters; the smaller bedrooms tucked under the eaves, each with antiques, delightful fabrics, and well-chosen items of china or cut glass, silver, or embroidery. The chef, Robert Jones, uses only the finest ingredients and his food is beautifully presented on delicate white Wedgwood china.

The house was the property of one family for over four hundred years. On the death of the last of the line, the contents were sold, and demolition threatened. Vandals stole the lead from the roof, so that the lovely, gracefully curving staircase to the right of the hall became a rushing torrent every time it rained. Rescued by a preservation order, the house was eventually bought by the Smedleys. Some of the original fixtures never left, or have been returned. The library book-shelves were sold to the USA, but an export license was refused; kitchenware, sold for pennies to someone in the village, will now form part of an exhibition when the original basement kitchens are restored. The 1770 portrait of the household servants by Thomas Beech, sold in 1956, has recently been willed back to the house by its buyer, and hangs again in the yellow dining room. This shows the housekeeper, who is supposed to have murdered the little stillroom maid (also portrayed) for love of the bailiff, one of the two male servants in the picture. It is the maid who still, it is said, haunts the upper floors of the house, quietly walking about, opening and shutting doors, never seen, never malevolent, but very much there. She is undisturbed by the restoration of the twenty bedrooms.

The Smedleys, totally undaunted by their Herculean task, have put the finishing touches to the rooms, which are impeccably maintained, and are now replanting the gardens to the plans drawn up by Humphry Repton, the famous landscape designer, in 1792. At a time when so many great country houses are in decay, Ston Easton has taken on a glorious new lease of life.

Opposite and above: every detail of these magnificent rooms repays attention. Overleaf: the stately exterior and antique-filled interiors are immaculately maintained.

STON EASTON PARK, Ston Easton, Nr Bath, Avon BA3 4DF. **Tel.** Chewton Mendip (076 121) 631. **Telex** 444738 A/B AVOSTL G. **Owners** Peter and Christine Smedley. **Open** All year. **Rooms** 20, incl. 10 twin, 1 single, 1 double, 7 four posters, 1 suite, all with bathroom, color TV, radio and direct-dial phone. **Facilities** Hall, Saloon, drawing room, library, 2 dining rooms, private yellow dining room. 25-acre parklands, river, billiard room. **Restrictions** No children under 12, dogs by prior arrangement only. **Terms** Expensive. **Credit cards** All major cards. **Getting there** M4, Exit 18, A46 to Bath, A39, A37 to Ston Easton. About 2 hrs. **Helicopter landing** Yes (same day). **Of local interest** Bath, Bristol. Wells, Bradford-on-Avon, Glastonbury, Cheddar Gorge, Mendip Hills. **Whole day expeditions** Stonehenge, Avebury, Stourhead, etc. Information sheet available. **Refreshments** King's Head, Litton; Miners Arms, Priddy. **Dining out** Parsonage, Farrington Gurney; No 3 Dining Room, Glastonbury; Popjoys, Bath; Hole in the Wall, Bath (see p. 63).

Good cooking and a relaxed atmosphere

A private country house until bought by Stephen and Penny Ross, Homewood Park was built mainly between the mid-18th and mid-19th centuries, although its cellars are much older. Stephen and Penny, busy with their Bath restaurant, Popjoys, had never meant to run a hotel, but when they saw the house they knew they had to buy it. They have already won back the garden, which has an arboretum and flourishing herbaceous borders, and have increased the number of bedrooms to fifteen: they feel this is the maximum to which they can give good personal attention while not neglecting their young family.

I was sure that I was going to enjoy my stay at Homewood Park even before I saw it, because the letters and telephone calls exchanged during booking had been so welcoming. Drawing up in front of the curiously ancient porch (filched, perhaps, by some previous owner from the Abbey ruins nearby), I was hardly out of my car before a cheerful girl appeared, knowing exactly whom to expect, and organized a young man to carry up my bags. This was just as well, for my room was at the very top of the house. The reward for climbing all the stairs, pausing from time to time to examine the attractive pictures, was the spectacular view from the dormer window over lovely rolling countryside. It was a most appealing room. A six-feet-wide double bed on a low dais had a canopy which followed the slope of the ceiling and a bedhead of matching cushions suspended from a brass rod. The pale orange, yellow, and pink of its delightful honeysuckle-pattern fabric were echoed in the colors of the wallpaper. Pale apple-green wall-to-wall carpeting set everything off pleasingly. The bathroom was also a delight, in solid golden modern oak,

with plenty of surfaces for toiletries. It had cheerful green plants, a shower boosted by a pump for good pressure, and a tub backed by white tiles embossed with a raised pattern of fruit. Scattered throughout the house are bronzes by a family friend, David Backhouse, which may be purchased.

Dinner was excellent: spinach soup with freshly baked bread faintly flavored with rosemary was followed by venison with redcurrants, braised lettuce, new potatoes, and firm courgettes, and a wonderful chocolate soufflé. The quality of the wine-list will be much appreciated by connoisseurs. The young staff are enthusiastic, dedicated, and friendly and there is a feeling of welcoming informality about the place that is particularly attractive. A frequent comment I heard was "Homewood Park is not as formal and grand as some places near Bath, but I really *like* it!"

Opposite and above: the gardens at Homewood Park are as lovely as the charming interiors.

HOMEWOOD PARK HOTEL, Hinton Charterhouse, Bath, Avon BA3 6BB. **Tel.** Limpley Stoke (022 122) 3731 and 2643. **Telex** No. **Owners** Stephen and Penny Ross. **Open** All year, except 24 Dec.–14 Jan. **Rooms** 15 double, all with bathroom, phone, radio, color TV. **Facilities** Bar, drawing room, 2 dining rooms, conference room, 10-acre grounds, tennis court, arboretum. **Restrictions** No dogs. **Credit cards** All major cards. **Terms** Medium. **Getting there** M4, off at Exit 18 to Bath, from which take A36 (Warminster road) for $5\frac{1}{2}$ miles. Turn L (signposted

Sharpstone). Hotel is first L turning. About $2\frac{1}{2}$ hrs. **Helicopter landing** Yes (2 days notice). **Of local interest** Bath, Stonehenge, Avebury, Marlborough, Salisbury. **Whole day expeditions** Hardy's Dorset, Mendip Hills, and Wells. **Refreshments** Haunch of Venison, Salisbury; Whitd Hart, Castle Combe; White Hart, Ford. **Dining out** Ston Easton Park, Ston Easton (see p. 69); Hole in the Wall, Bath (see p. 63); Hunstrete House, Hunstrete (see p. 65).

Gourmet dining in an old-world hotel

Visitors arriving in Taunton in late spring will probably find The Castle Hotel smothered in wisteria blossom. It is an oasis of quiet in the center of a busy town, and faces a wide square. The remains of its Norman moat and keep are now a charming garden with flowering cherry trees, spring bulbs, and a green lawn. Once inside its thick walls, you could be in the heart of the country. The history of the castle goes back over twelve hundred years, and it has seen crowned heads passing through since Anglo-Saxon times. It became a hotel some three hundred years ago. From the first it was a notable hostelry and stage-coach stop. It has continued to entertain royalty, including Queen Victoria and the present Queen Mother.

From the moment that your bags are taken by a uniformed hall porter, you are looked after with professional efficiency and West Country charm. Managing Director Christopher Chapman is no newcomer to the hotel business. His grandfather managed the London Savoy in its Edwardian heyday: the legendary parties he organized there before being tempted to New York by a salary "larger than the Prime Minister's" are still remembered with awe. Christopher Chapman's father and mother began the process of modernizing The Castle which he has continued, still with their help. The very comfortable bedrooms are not only well designed, but have splendid bathrooms with efficient showers. Each room has a different décor, some using antiques, velvets, and brocades, others chintz, wicker, and bamboo. One tower room has a tall arched bedhead which echoes its arched window. The barman in the welcoming Rose Room is swift and efficient, and not only remembers which drink you ordered last time, but also your name and room number. The restaurant is formal in an almost thirties way; it has a high ceiling, tall windows draped with heavy velvet curtains, starched white tablecloths, chandeliers, and waitresses in black dresses and caps.

The chef, Christopher Oakes, is outstanding. I ate green ogen melon, of peak ripeness, peeled and sliced into a fan and surrounded by morello cherry sauce sharpened with black pepper and fresh limes. Veal fillet, tender and juicy, in a butter and herb sauce, was accompanied by calf's liver in a light pastry case. Courgettes, new potatoes, and tiny green beans were exactly right for firmness and seasoning. A cinnamon soufflé – daringly punctured on serving to pour in drambuie cream – was followed by coffee and hand-made chocolates. A meal to remember in a hotel which was a total delight.

Opposite and above: neat flower gardens in the Norman moat, four-poster beds, and afternoon tea in this especially welcoming hotel.

THE CASTLE HOTEL, Castle Green, Taunton, Somerset TA1 1NF. **Tel.** Taunton (0823) 72671. **Telex** 46488 A/B CASTLE G. **Owners** The Chapman family. Managing Director, Christopher Chapman. **Open** All year. **Rooms** 35, incl. 1 large suite, and 4 smaller suites, all with bathroom (tub and shower), radio, color TV, phone. **Facilities** Lift, Rose Room with bar, Oak Room, restaurant, 1½-acre grounds with garden (incl. Norman well). **Restrictions** Dogs by arrangement only and not in public rooms. **Terms** Medium. **Credit cards** All major cards. **Getting there** M4, M5, Exit 25 to center of Taunton. About 2¾ hrs. **Helicopter landing** Yes (2 days notice). **Of local interest** Exmoor and Lorna Doone country, Dorset and Thomas Hardy country, King Arthur's Glastonbury, Wells, Stourhead. Hotel provides excellent touring information and maps. **Whole day expeditions** Thorough exploration of one of the above! **Refreshments** Tea Clipper, Milton Abbas; The Settle, Frome; Simonsbath House, Simonsbath. **Dining out** Nothing nearby.

Far from the madding crowd

If you arrive at Boscundle Manor during the afternoon, you may find Mary Flint happily weeding her beloved garden. She will not be in the least discomposed at being surprised in her gardening clothes, and will cheerfully summon her husband, Andrew, who will help with your bags, settle you into your room, and prepare a welcoming cup of tea. Anybody who has recently been staying at very formal establishments may find this unnerving, but they need be in no doubt about the comfort of the simple bedrooms, or the excellence of the meals served in the dining room, which gleams with polished mahogany and shining silverware.

Andrew Flint, impeccably besuited, orchestrates swift and efficient service, is highly knowledgeable about wines, and has compiled an excellent and very reasonable wine-list. He is justly proud of the delicious Stilton soup, sole Véronique, duckling with cherry and brandy sauce, traditional desserts with Cornish clotted cream, and other expertly prepared dishes, which have won high praise for Mary from Michelin Inspectors as well as from local gourmets. Andrew himself is no novice in the kitchen – he cooks all the breakfasts.

The Flints are escapees from a fast-track London life. Andrew had a senior post with an internationally famous group of city chartered accountants; Mary used to help run a prestigious secretarial agency. Visiting Cornwall, they saw and fell in love with Boscundle Manor and its garden, then a wilderness. They do not know a great deal about the history of the house, except that the very thick walls of the cottage that was the original building on the site suggest medieval origins. This now forms part of their breakfast room. Part of the Manor is probably Georgian, and the whole building rambles about in the haphazard way of houses that have been added to over the centuries. A pleasant small bar has been built at the rear, and the Flints have filled their home with an intriguing assortment of antiques. Paintings by their friend Fred Yates have been hung throughout; his charming Cornish scenes (rather in the style of L. S. Lowry) are in many important collections worldwide and may be purchased here. The garden is the Flints' great passion, and as well as planting many trees, shrubs, and flowers, they have also constructed a swimming pool, terrace, and summerhouse. With their own hands they moved massive granite blocks to form flights of steps and levelled terraces, and they have also laid out a croquet lawn. They have recently bought another cottage on which they are working. Enthusiastic, indefatigable, and welcoming hosts, it is hard to believe, after having spent only an evening with them, that one has not known them for years.

Opposite and above: Boscundle Manor has an atmosphere of rural peace both inside and out.

BOSCUNDLE MANOR, Tregrehan, St Austell, Cornwall PL25 3RL. **Tel.** Par (072 681) 3557. **Telex** No. **Owners** Andrew and Mary Flint. **Open** All year, except Christmas–mid-Feb. Restaurant closed to *non*-residents Suns. and bank holidays. Lunch for arranged parties only. **Rooms** 5 double, 2 single, all with bathroom (2 with tub, 5 with shower), phone, color TV, radio. **Facilities** Drawing room, bar, restaurant, conservatory, 2-acre hillside garden, $7\frac{1}{2}$ acres of adjoining woodland (with old tin mine), croquet, heated outdoor pool. **Restrictions** No dogs in public rooms. **Terms** Moderate. **Credit cards** Visa/Amex/Access. **Getting there** M4 to Bristol, M5 to Exeter, A38 to Dobwalls, A390 to St Austell. About 6 hrs. **Helicopter landing** No. **Of local interest** Fowey, Megavissey, and Roseland peninsular. Coastal path walks. Many Celtic remains; many local artists. Cothele estate, Lanhydrock, Trewithin, and Trelissick gardens. **Whole day expeditions** Bodmin Moor (Jamaica Inn at Bolventor), St Ives, Zenor, Cap Cornwall, St Michael's Mount. **Refreshments** Pandora Inn, Mylor Bridge; Roseland Inn, Philleigh; Rising Sun, St Mawes. **Dining out** The Riverside, Helford (see p. 79); Food for Thought, Fowey; The Fish Restaurant, Padstow.

A taste of Cornwall

A quiet haven for country-lovers and fishermen, an unforgettable experience for gourmets, The Riverside combines understated English charm with delicious French provincial cuisine.

Two small whitewashed cottages on the leafy slopes of a quiet creek that opens into the sea, The Riverside is in a remote, unspoilt corner of England, far from the noise and the traffic, where wildflowers which have vanished from much of England still bloom in profusion in the spring. It is on the edge of Helford, the picturesque village that Daphne du Maurier used as a setting for her famous novel *Frenchman's Creek*. There is a shop, a post office, a handful of assorted houses and cottages, and a thatched waterside pub, The Shipwright's Arms, sometime haunt of Prince Andrew. The windows of The Riverside, with their deep-cushioned window seats in the three-foot-thick medieval cob walls, look out over dinghies at anchor in the creek. The six bedrooms are snug, warm, and have a cottagey simplicity, yet are surprisingly large; each one is different, and all have interesting books, prints, and ornaments. A sun-trap terrace has white porch furniture; there is a small, steep garden, with a great feeling of peace and tranquillity.

George Perry-Smith and Heather Crosbie first made their reputation for imaginative and superbly flavored French-provincial-inspired cooking at The Hole in the Wall in Bath (see page 63). They moved to Cornwall some years ago for the mild climate, the quiet country living, and the superb selection of fresh ingredients. The lamb, salmon, and lobsters they use are all local, and most of the vegetables are grown on the slopes above the hotel. Their hospitality is relaxed and generous. Breakfasts are continental, ample, and self-service, with fresh-baked breads and croissants, homemade jams and marmalade. Dinner begins with a memorable cold table, from which you may browse at will, adding as many further courses as you wish, and George himself will probably wander through from the kitchen to enquire modestly whether you are enjoying your meal, as though the low-ceilinged restaurant were not filled with international gourmets who had journeyed to this far end of England to eat the seabass and mushroom cutlets, or bisque with great chunks of lobster, or fresh salmon with currants and ginger, or the St Emilion au chocolat. The wine-list is expertly compiled and reasonably priced.

Since comfort, quiet, a friendly but unfussy welcome, and outstanding cooking, combined in a delightful rural setting are hard to find, and since there are only six bedrooms, one must always book well in advance. From here one may tour Cornwall, take long walks along the river, fish, sail, or simply have fun "messing about in boats."

*Opposite: a farmer toils in the fields above The Riverside.
Above: the hotel's rooms are quietly comfortable.*

THE RIVERSIDE, Helford, Helston, Cornwall TR1 26JU. **Tel.** Manaccan (032 623) 443. **Telex** No. **Owners** George Perry-Smith and Heather Crosbie. **Open** End March–end Oct. Restaurant closed to *non*-residents Sun. and Mon. **Rooms** 6 double, 3 in each cottage. All with bathroom (tubs not showers), TV, tea/coffee making tray. No phones in bedrooms. **Facilities** Small lounge for residents, restaurant, bar/breakfast room, sun terrace. Light lunches and picnics for residents on request. **Restrictions** No dogs. **Terms** Moderate. Meals are at a reduced price for residents and children; special meals for children. **Credit cards** No. Personal checks or cash only. **Getting there** M4, M5, A30, A39, A394 to Helston. From Helston, A3083 (signposted Lizard) through RNAS Culdrose. Turn L (signposted St Keverne), L again at sign for Helford. Down steep track into public carpark on R. Riverside is on L. About 6 hrs. **Helicopter landing** No. **Of local interest** Beaches, fishing, walking, sailing. Godolphin House, St Michael's Mount, Trelowarren House, castles at Falmouth and St Mawes, gardens at Trelissick and Glendurgan. Minnack open-air theater. Guild of Ten (local craftsmen) at Truro. **Whole day expeditions** It is very rewarding to follow the coast roads and drop down steep narrow tracks to tiny fishing villages. Cornwall attracts many artists, potters, and weavers, most of whom welcome visitors to their studios. **Refreshments** Roseland Inn, Philleigh; Shipwright's Arms, Helford; Rising Sun, St Mawes. **Dining out** Boscundle Manor, St Austell (see p. 77).

Sturminster Newton
Dorset

Explore Thomas Hardy's native county

This is the perfect place to stay for devotees of Thomas Hardy's novels who wish to explore his Dorset, or visit his birthplace at Higher Brockhampton, or walk on "Egdon" (Winfrith) Heath, or stay in Sturminster Newton, where he wrote *The Return of the Native*; it is also ideal for those who wish to climb the immense ramparts of Maiden Castle, built four thousand years ago, or buy handthrown bowls from Bernard Leach's grandson at Muchelney Pottery, or stand in Wareham's tiny Saxon church of St Martin in front of the effigy of Lawrence of Arabia slumbering in Arab robes, head on a camel saddle.

Prideaux-Brunes have lived at Plumber Manor for over three hundred years. Their portraits hang in an upstairs gallery in the square Jacobean house. Richard Prideaux-Brune, Old Harrovian and A Character, will welcome you in the stone-floored entrance hall, which has a graceful staircase, accumulated family bric-à-brac (including a stuffed Greenland falcon), and bowls of fresh flowers. He will be on hand later to serve you drinks from the well-stocked bar in the sitting room. The delightful restaurant, favored by the local gentry, is presided over by the chef, his brother Brian, who produces reliably delicious food from a reassuringly short menu based on daily deliveries of fresh produce. Crab with melon, loin of pork with calvados, cream, and apple, and almond meringue with brandy and apricot sauce were excellent. It was hard to decide between the mouth-watering selection on the dessert-trolley, all prepared daily on the premises. The bedrooms in the main house are comfortable and convenient, those in the stable block larger and yet more splendid to compensate for the minor inconvenience of walking the few yards to the main house (golf umbrellas provided). As Richard Prideaux-Brune says, "This is

all part of our house, and we would not want, or put up with, shoddy workmanship."

As well as strolling in the 300-acre estate, keen gardeners will enjoy a visit to nearby Stourhead, probably England's finest landscape garden, or to Montacute House, which has a splendid formal Elizabethan garden stocked with strains of traditional roses. On the coast not far away is Lyme Regis, whose lovely surroundings and chalk cliffs are the haunt of fossil hunters. Scenes in Jane Austen's *Persuasion* and John Fowles's *The French Lieutenant's Woman* are set here.

Plumber Manor is not there to cosset and indulge its guests. It provides an excellent dinner, a comfortable bed, a hearty English breakfast and advice, if required, about what to see. After this guests set off for the day to explore Dorset, returning in the evening to the Prideaux-Brune family waiting to hear of the day's exploits.

Opposite and above: the discreet driveway leads to a country gentleman's attractive home.

PLUMBER MANOR, Sturminster Newton, Dorset, DT10 2AF. **Tel.** Sturminster Newton (0258) 72507. **Telex** No. **Owner** Richard Prideaux-Brune. **Open** All year, except 2 weeks in Nov. and all Feb. **Rooms** 12 double, with bathroom, color TV, phone. **Facilities** Sitting room/bar, drawing room, 3 dining rooms, 300-acre estate, croquet, hard tennis court. **Restrictions** No dogs, no children. **Terms** Moderate. **Credit cards** Not accepted. Personal checks only. **Getting there** From London M3, A30, A303 to Amesbury, A354 to Blandford Forum, A357/B3092 to Sturminster Newton. About 2½ hrs. **Helicopter landing** No. **Of local interest** Valley of River Piddle, Montacute, Stourhead, Tolpuddle, Lyme Regis, Blandford Forum, Dorchester. **Whole day expeditions** Salisbury, Wareham, Corfe Castle and Studland Peninsular. **Refreshments** Brace of Pheasants, Plush; Fiddleford Inn, Fiddleford. **Dining out** The Priory, Wareham.

Sophisticated splendors

The New Forest – new that is for William the Conqueror – was a royal hunting preserve, ruthlessly formed by flattening several Saxon villages, driving off the inhabitants, and imposing savage penalties on trespassers. For disturbing the deer, blinding; for shooting arrows at the deer, a hand cut off; for killing a deer, death. The site of Chewton Glen Hotel was by then already inhabited. Happily the laws governing the area are no longer so brutal, though many medieval forestry regulations still survive. The present house on the site was owned in the mid-19th century by the brother of Captain Marryat, author of *The Children of the New Forest*, who spent some time here, and from whose books the names of many of the rooms are taken. Chewton Glen is now a world-famous hotel, as sophisticated and in tune with the life of the international traveller as any of the better London hotels, and yet it has not lost the friendly and welcoming atmosphere of a gracious private house in the country. Bedrooms are sunny and elegantly chintzy, designed for comfort and furnished with taste, and all possessing that (for England) rare delight, a thermostatically controlled shower. Many bedrooms have balconies. The suites in the old stable are on two floors, and have a tiny garden and an extra bathroom each. The view over the main gardens is of smooth green lawns, stone urns overflowing with colorful cascades of flowers, neat gravel walks, a terraced pool, and a backdrop of trees. Downstairs, François Rossi presides with Gallic charm over the formal cocktail bar, where you ponder your choice of dishes and await the summons of Tony Ferrario, the Restaurant Manager. The dining room has walls the soft red of the blush of a ripe peach, gleaming white table-cloths, and at night is lit by tall brass

candlesticks with heavy glass shades. I found that a hot mousse of mushrooms in a port sauce was delicate and finely seasoned, a turban of assorted fish in a lobster butter sauce melted in the mouth, and ratatouille, separate courgettes, and potatoes faintly flavored with artichoke were all perfect. A slice of soft Italian meringue with slightly crunchy almost caramelized crystallized orange crumbled into it, flavored with Cointreau and served chilled, and a cup of excellent coffee, completed a superb meal. Chef Pierre Chevillard richly deserves his Michelin Guide star. The owner, Martin Skan, has a fine team of managers (David Brochett and Jo Simonini) and department heads, many of whom have been with him for anything up to eighteen years. It is their attention to every detail concerning the comfort of the guest that makes Chewton Glen such a very impressive place in which to stay.

Opposite: Chewton Glen's front door has welcomed many international guests eager to sample its famous cuisine (above). Overleaf: the colorful hallway and luxurious rooms are complemented by the magnificent grounds.

CHEWTON GLEN HOTEL, New Milton, Hampshire BH25 6QS. **Tel.** Highcliffe (04252) 5341. **Telex** 41456 A/B CHGLEN. **Owner** Martin Skan. **Open** All year. **Rooms** 33 double, 11 suites, all with bathroom (tub and shower each), color TV, direct-dial phone, radio. **Facilities** Bar, bar/lounge with pianist, 2 other lounges, private dining room, private board room, restaurant, boutique, snooker room, heated outdoor pool (summer only), all-weather tennis court, croquet, putting, 30-acre grounds, incl. valley walk to sea and beach. Chauffeur service. **Restrictions** No dogs; no children under 7. **Terms** Medium. Special weekend programs arranged. **Credit cards** All major cards accepted. **Getting there** M3, M27 to Exit 1 (marked Lyndhurst). After Lyndhurst follow signs to A35 (marked Christchurch and Bournemouth). After 11 miles, take L turning to Walkford and Highcliffe. Hotel is signposted just after Walkford. About 2 hrs. **Helicopter landing** Yes ("a few days notice"). **Of local interest** Golf, sailing, cruising, riding, fishing, and horse-drawn cart rides can all be arranged with notice. Broadlands, Exbury Gardens, Beaulieu (and Motor Museum). Mary Rose Museum. **Whole day expeditions** Winchester, Salisbury, Hardy's Dorset, etc. See hotel's own guide. **Refreshments** Red Lion, Boldre; Rose and Thistle, Rockbourne; Fox Inn, Ansty. **Dining out** Old Manor House, Romsey.

A famous architect's costly showpiece

Surrounded in spring by a sea of pink and white apple blossom, Little Thakeham looks like a typical early English stone manor house, with later additions in red brick hung with Sussex tiles. But appearances deceive: though Tudor in style, with a Great Hall, Minstrels' Gallery, huge fireplace, and upstairs Long Gallery for exercise on rainy days, Little Thakeham was designed by the notable architect Sir Edwin Lutyens at the turn of this century for a wealthy Brighton businessman. Lutyens used only the finest materials and most skilled craftsmen, with glorious results. Throughout the house are solid oak, shining quarry tiles, hand-crafted iron door hinges and latches, and polished stone floors. The garden, laid out by the famous Gertrude Jekyll, has rose walks – note the millstones set into the paths – shrubberies, grassy recreation areas for tennis and croquet, and a pergola leading the eye to the orchards and woods beyond. All this was to be for a family of five with thirteen servants, but unfortunately the lavish use of only the best bankrupted the businessman.

The present owners, Tim and Pauline Ratcliff, have supplemented the original bedrooms by converting day and night nurseries and attics into delightful individual bedchambers, with charming wallpapers, attractive fabrics, and modern bathrooms. They have almost finished restoring the garden (adding a swimming pool discreetly), but have not replaced the eighty-year-old climbing roses, chosen by the designer. They have hunted out furniture contemporary with the house, and even found the Lutyens-designed original sideboard, now back in its proper place in the dining room.

Tim Ratcliff feels very strongly about using only the best English ingredients cooked in the delicious traditional manner. Lobster, halibut, and sole come from the south coast, and the famous Southdown lamb is raised only a few miles away. There are Hampshire melons, wild game from Sussex, and thick yellow cream from a nearby Jersey herd. Local market gardens and the surrounding orchards provide fresh vegetables and fruit; herbs are from the gardens. The wine-list is a connoisseur's selection, and includes some exceptional vintages. Sitting with fellow guests in front of the big log fire after an excellent meal, I found them unanimous in their praise of the food and of the relaxing house-party atmosphere. The next morning, faced with pouring rain, people contentedly curled up with magazines in the comfortable armchairs, or happily wandered through the spacious house, examining with delight its features and contents. On fine days there is all the marvellous Hampshire and Sussex countryside to explore as well as Roman Chichester's medieval cathedral and modern boutiques, and Brighton's fantastic Royal Pavilion, gracious Regency terraces, and intricate Lanes, a lure for all antique hunters.

Opposite, above, and overleaf: Little Thakeham house and gardens are the creation of two geniuses – Edwin Lutyens and Gertrude Jekyll – and their heritage has been lovingly preserved.

LITTLE THAKEHAM, Merrywood Lane, Storrington, West Sussex RH20 3HE. **Tel.** Storrington (09066) 4416. **Telex** No. **Owners** Tim and Pauline Ratcliff. **Open** All year, except 10 days following 24 Dec. **Rooms** 9 double, all with bathroom, color TV, direct-dial phone, radio. **Facilities** Bar, lounge, dining room, pool, grass tennis court, croquet lawn, 5-acre grounds. Courtesy cars by arrangement. **Restrictions** Children at management's discretion. No dogs. **Terms** Medium. **Credit cards** All major cards (personal checks preferred). **Getting there** A24. After Ashington, watch for Thakeham turning on R. Bear R at fork. Hotel is about $1\frac{1}{2}$ miles from turning. About $1\frac{1}{2}$ hrs. **Helicopter landing** Yes (24 hrs notice). **Of local interest** Horse racing at Goodwood. Arundel Castle, Petworth House, Brighton, Lewes, Chichester. **Whole day expeditions** Winchester, Chartwell (Churchill's home), Leonards Lee gardens, Gilbert White's Selborne. **Refreshments** Harrow, Steep (nr Petersfield); Bridge, Amberley. **Dining out** Manley's, Storrington. NB Bookings of 2 nights or longer preferred.

Live like a lord

Newick Park, home of Viscount Brentford, is not a hotel as such, and you cannot drive up to the front door expecting to find a bed for that night. It is a member of the Heritage Circle, a small group of owners of some of England's loveliest historic houses who welcome visitors wishing to experience day-to-day life in what is essentially a family home. Arrangements must be made well in advance, by telephone or letter, with Lady Brentford.

Newick Park is a handsome 18th-century mansion whose famous garden includes shrubs brought from China at the end of the last century, and 300-year-old sweet chestnut trees. From the moment you arrive you are a family guest. There is no drinks book to sign, no menu, no extras except any telephone calls or whatever you might wish to leave for the staff. Your account will be left for you discreetly in the Visitors' Book which you sign on departure. The pleasant bedrooms mostly have names acquired over the years. Mine was the Tulip Room, with tall windows looking over parkland, an extremely comfortable bed, central heating, and a space heater, electric blanket, and hot-water bottle for a sudden cold snap. It had pink walls, rose-motif chintz, its own bathroom across the corridor and the sort of collection of varied antiques found only in English country houses. Do not expect television, radio, or telephone in your room – they are available elsewhere in the house.

Dinner is served formally in the elegantly proportioned dining room at a long polished table graced with flowers and family silver. Crispin Brentford sits at its head, listening with a lawyer's courteous attention to the conversation. Behind him hangs the life-size portrait of his grandfather Sir William Joynson-Hicks, First Viscount, sometime Home Secretary, and for long a political rival of Sir Winston Churchill. Another likeness is of a lady who scandalized the family by eloping through the pantry window with the gentleman whose picture hangs beside hers. Gill Brentford serves traditional English

dishes, delicious as only home cooking can be: smoked fish, tender lamb, beef, or duck from the estate, locally grown vegetables, and family-favorite desserts of trifle, pies, or tarts, with fresh fruit from their orchards and perfectly selected cheeses to follow.

The hosts tend to retire early, as Lord Brentford is a partner in the family law firm, and Lady Brentford assists in a commodity trading company, another family business. Having only recently inherited the estate, they are also very busy improving the grounds. They are charming, friendly, and attentive hosts, with an international outlook (their eldest daughter has been educated in the USA). A footnote: if necessary, arrangements can be made to accommodate chauffeurs in the village.

Opposite and above: attractive gardens and gracious interiors at Newick Park add to the pleasure of sampling the daily life of the aristocracy.

NEWICK PARK, Newick, East Sussex BN8 4SB. **Tel.** Newick (082 572) 2915. **Telex** No. **Owners** Viscount and Viscountess Brentford. **Open** All year, except Christmas and Easter. **Rooms** 10 twin, 2 single, 10 bathrooms (6 en suite, 4 shared). No TV or phone in bedrooms. **Facilities** Hall, drawing room, library, dining room. Guest phone and TV. Pool, tennis courts, croquet. **Restrictions** No children under 7; no dogs. **Terms** Medium. **Credit cards** Visa/Amex. **Getting there** M23, A23, E on A272 to Newick. About 1½ hrs. **Helicopter landing** Yes (2 days notice). **Of local interest** Glyndebourne Opera (May to August), Knole, Lewes, Brighton. **Whole day expeditions** Canterbury, Bodiam Castle, Leeds Castle, Sissinghurst and Scotney gardens. **Refreshments** Blackboys, Blackboys; Rose and Crown, Fletching. **Dining out** Gravetye Manor, nr East Grinstead; Hubbards, Newick.

For lovers of opera and the countryside

Building began on The Priory eighty years before Columbus discovered America. By some lucky stroke of fate, the thousand acres of glorious Sussex countryside that have always made up its estate have escaped development, and the medieval stone and half-timbered building stands on a hillside looking out over unspoilt woods and fields with not another house in sight beyond its own small cluster of farm buildings. Seized by Henry VIII from the Augustinian monks who built it, and given by him to his Attorney General, it was sold then and there to the ancestors of Peter Dunn, in whose family it has remained ever since.

The slightly crumbling ancient stone doorway, the dark beams of the low ceilings, the huge fireplace big enough to roast a sheep in, are still there. Peter Dunn and his interior designer wife, Jane, have preserved the character of the house, while adding the modern comforts of central heating and efficient bathrooms. The fresh countryfied bedrooms have all those small extra items that Peter knew from his life as an international businessman would be helpful for the traveller.

The abbot's brick-floored private apartments have become the restaurant, notable for its use of fresh local ingredients. Romney Marsh lamb is roasted with a hint of rosemary, stuffed with carrot and apple, and served by friendly local village girls, who leave covered dishes of vegetables on the table for you to serve yourself. When you are enjoying the homemade sorbets, or rich chocolate marquise, remember to leave room to sample the wide choice of regional cheeses, all British. The selection of wines is exceptionally good.

International opera lovers come from all over the world to the Glyndebourne Festival, held in the famous country house theater a few miles away; for this the Dunns offer a traditional lavish picnic packed in a wicker hamper. Later in the year, Land Rovers, dogs, guns, and rods are available for guests who, accompanied by Peter Dunn or a gamekeeper, would like a day's shooting or fishing.

Those interested in the history of the Priory can trace the outline of the ruined chapel, or stroll along the track made by the monks dragging building stone from the nearby quarry. You might also ask Peter Dunn about Henry VIII's Deed of Gift, and the story of the monks' bones!

Opposite and above: staying in the medieval Priory allows you to sample English country food at its best – this marvellous selection of cheese is entirely British.

THE PRIORY COUNTRY HOUSE HOTEL, Rushlake Green, Heathfield, East Sussex, TN21 9RG. **Tel.** Rushlake Green (0435) 830553. **Telex** 957210 A/B RLP G. **Owners** Jane and Peter Dunn. **Open** All year, except 25 Dec.–12 Jan. **Rooms** 11 double, 1 single. All with bathroom, color TV, phone, and radio. 6 of the rooms in a converted oast house. 3 other rooms at Stone House for Glyndebourne visitors (May to August), with same facilities. **Facilities** 2 drawing rooms, 2 dining rooms, small conference facilities. Glyndebourne visits, shooting, fishing, and private visits to stately homes arranged. 4-acre garden with croquet. 1000-acre estate. **Restrictions** No children under 9; no dogs in public rooms. **Terms** Moderate. **Credit cards** No. Traveller's or personal checks in sterling or dollars on UK or US banks. **Getting there** A23/M23, Exit 10, A264 towards East Grinstead, A22 towards Uckfield, turn off L at Maresfield on A272 to Buxted. At T junction turn R to Heathfield. From Heathfield A265/B2096 towards Battle. At Three Cups pub (on R), turn R. Fork L after 1 mile, follow lane to hotel sign. About 2 hrs. **Helicopter landing** Yes (24 hrs notice). **Of local interest** Burwash, Hurstmonceaux, Battle, Bodiam Castle, Rye, Sissinghurst gardens. **Whole day expeditions** Chartwell (Churchill's home), Knole, gardens at Scotney, Leonards Lee, and Nymans; Canterbury, Sandwich (famous golf course). **Refreshments** Horse and Groom, Rushlake Green; William the Conqueror, Rye harbor; Star Inn, Heathfield. **Dining out** Blacksmith's Restaurant, Battle; Gravetye Manor, East Grinstead.

An architectural jig-saw

Stone Green Hall is a collector's item for those who like unusual houses and interesting owners. The original building was a modest 16th-century red-brick cottage, and each owner down the centuries seems to have added something: a Georgian wing with a tall, arched window and elegant carved staircase; a gracious hall, its floor patterned in black and white like a chess board, and spacious Edwardian reception rooms. A past chairman of Sotheby's added a splendid Portland-Stone-floored dining room and a lofty glass conservatory filled with camellia bushes now 15 feet high. The bathrooms were created at a stroke by converting every other huge bedroom into a luxurious dressing room-cum-bathroom – the Californian wife of the last owner installed in one a four-poster *bathtub*.

The present owners, the Kempstons, have contented themselves with restoring each part of the house to its original character, and are now turning their attention to the demanding but rewarding task of winning back the large formal garden to its former splendor, and re-establishing the kitchen and herb gardens. They have unearthed treasures: a totally overgrown gazebo at the end of the small lake and a rare Magnolia grandiflora hidden among the fruit trees in the orchard. A former owner opened the vista over pastureland by removing an old brick wall and digging a ha-ha, which has now become a stream patronized by friendly mallards. The Kempstons are busy improving their view by planting well-placed groves of trees.

James Kempston is an inspired, self-taught chef, whose goulash soup, fresh brill meunière with celeriac potatoes and mange-tout peas, and house ginger pudding, steeped in ginger wine and topped with heavy whipped cream, rival the creations of top London chefs. His Latvian wife, Ingrid, has filled the house with well-chosen pictures, books, and china (do not miss the downstairs cloakroom). Sometimes a group of friends will take over the house completely, which then becomes as it were their private establishment. The solitary visitor, however, is not neglected, as I discovered when I arrived one cold winter evening to find myself the only guest. A table was laid for me before a roaring fire, with double damask, gleaming silver, and flowers, and the next morning I had one of the best breakfasts I can remember eating, including James Kempston's amazing porridge.

At weekends the restaurant is well supported by local inhabitants, and the Kempstons arrange special evenings to sample the food of different nations. On occasions they hold a dinner dance, and guests waltz sedately to a piano by candlelight under the low-beamed ceiling in the most ancient part of the house.

Opposite: Gardens, conservatory, and an elegant Georgian stairway are part of a beautiful ensemble. The food (above) is equally memorable.

STONE GREEN HALL, Mersham, Nr Ashford, Kent TN25 7HE. **Tel.** Aldington (023 372) 418. **Telex** No. **Owners** James and Ingrid Kempston. **Open** All year, except Christmas and Feb. **Rooms** 3 double (king- or queen-sized beds), 1 twin, all with color TV, radio, bathroom. Twin has shower as well as tub. No phones in bedrooms. **Facilities** Writing room, drawing room, conservatory, private dining room, restaurant, 5-acre garden, lawn tennis, croquet. **Restrictions** No children under 12 in hotel or under 6 in restaurant. **Terms** Moderate. **Credit cards** Access/ Euro/Amex/Visa. **Getting there** M20 to Ashford (Exit 10), A20 s. After 3 miles take Mersham turning. In Mersham follow signs to Aldington. Hotel is on L, ½ mile on, past The Farriers Inn, a cricket ground, and over a small bridge. About 2 hrs. **Helicopter landing** No. **Of local interest** Cinque ports, Romney Marsh villages, Lyminge, Bishopsbourne, Barham, Chilham, gardens at Sissinghurst and Great Dixter, Leeds Castle. **Whole day expeditions** Canterbury, golf at Deal and Sandwich. **Refreshments** Three Chimneys, Beddenden; Flying Horse, Boughton Lees; White Horse, Chilham; Three Compasses, Sole. **Dining out** The Priory, Rushlake Green (see p. 93); Waterfield's, Canterbury; Paul's Restaurant, Folkestone.

Index